mkGandhi

The Educationist Par Excellence

mkgandhi
The Educationist Par Excellence

Onkar Singh Dewal

Ocean Books Pvt. Ltd.

ISO 9001:2015 Publishers

Published by
Ocean Books (P) Ltd.
4/19 Asaf Ali Road,
New Delhi-110 002 (INDIA)
e-mail: info@oceanbooks.in

ISBN 978-81-8430-316-2
M.K. Gandhi: The Educationist Par Excellence
by Onkar Singh Dewal

Edition
2025

Price
₹ 300.00 (Rupees Three Hundred only)

Printed at
Shree Sai Printers, Sahibabad

To

My Grand Children

Snigdha and Shashank

Daughter and Son of

Dr. O.P. Dewal and Mrs. Gunbala Dewal

Mikita and Ashvin

Daughter and Son of

Sanjay Roharia and Mrs. Anand Roharia

Devangana

Daughter of

Harsh Verdhan Dewal and Mrs. Shashi Dewal

Preface

When Prof. J.S. Rajput was the Chairperson of National Council for Teacher Education (NCTE) (1994-1999) he brought out a book on Gandhiji's views, ideas and philosophy on education entitled, **'Gandhi on Education'**. The book was greatly appreciated all over India and abroad. The contents of the book were grouped under seven parts.

- Meaning of Education
- Aims of Education
- Experiments on Education in South Africa
- Experiments on Education in India
- Education at various stages and related questions
- Thoughts on various aspects of Education
- On Students and Teachers

During that period, 1994-1999, I was also associated with NCTE. Indirectly and in a marginal way I witnessed the growth of this book and visited, a few times, Gujarat Vidyapeeth along with Prof. Rajput. I had occasion to meet Prof. Ram Lal Parikh who was then Vice Chancellor. He would tell us many inner stories and spoke of Gandhiji's insight on different educational processes. These occasions made me study Gandhiji's views on education.

In 2006 Prof. Rajput discussed with me an idea on, **Seven Social Ills**, of Mahatma Gandhi and desired that an in-depth probe in this area will be a stimulating task to illustrate how Gandhiji's mind saw main ills connected with politics, pleasure, education, science, commerce, wealth and worship.

When we discussed this point, an idea cropped up that there are also some pedagogical ills. I wrote a small article, Seven

Pedagogical Ills, under the title, *Towards Effective Teaching* (Eternal India, April 2010 pp. 80-90).

Many teacher educators and principals of teacher colleges had interactions with me on phone. While discussing the contents of this article I would also point out the massive importance of Gandhiji's Nai Taleem or Basic Education. I found that most of teacher educators only had limited understanding about Basic Education and its philosophy. This limited background of many teacher educators, teachers and educational administrators prompted me to write this book. It presents Gandhiji as an extraordinary teacher. His way of learning was deep and living; vibrant and pulsating. He always listened carefully and attentively. He observed keenly. He reflected deeply. He read with full understanding. But his journey on learning did not end there. He will himself experiment. In his discussion with Romain Rolland in 1931, he said, "I have learnt a little from history. **My way of learning is personal experience**".

We often pay lip tribute to Mahatma Ji. We have verbal praise for his economic philosophy. We pay hollow tribute to respect him but hardly follow his principles, his practices, his simplicity, in our lives. His service to secure India's freedom through non-violence means, his love for the untouchables, his efforts for Hindu-Muslim unity, his dream to empower villages, his economic ideas are recalled with respect in India and abroad on 2nd October but often forgotten on 3rd October. Moreover, we rarely have any comment about his contributions to the process of education; relating to its principles and practices.

Since 2009, Shastri Bhavan is bubbling with energy and enthusiasm and have offered mind boggling changes in the educational system. These ranges from introduction of the semester system, constituting an overarching body to look after higher education and research, inviting foreign universities to open their campus in India and many others.

The Planning Commission Member Narendra Jadhav, was of the view (Times of India 17.1.2011) that five educational bills may be cleared in 2011. They relate to creation of National Commission for Higher Education and Research (NCHER), Foreign Education Providers Bill, Educational Tribunal Bill, Accreditation Bill and Prohibition of Educational Malpractices Bill. Here, we hardly see any attempt to revive basic education or education for character. It seems that people do not see the relevance of views of M.K.G. on education. The objective of this book is to delve deep on the thought and practices of Gandhiji and see their significance. If we disregards his contributions to education we essentially disregard the, Father of Nation.

Hundreds of excellent books by world renowned writers like Romain Rolland, Louis Fisher, Dr. S. Radhakrishnan, J.B. Kriplani, V.K.R.V. Rao have been written illuminating the multiple aspects of personality of Mahatma Gandhi. He, himself, in his voluminous correspondence, speeches, brief notes had showed us the working of his inner mind. And yet thousands of more books need to be written on that person whose inner wealth of thought and feeling still remain an ocean unexplored; whose deeds were more than his words, who was greater than his deeds and truer than his surroundings. His creative approach, critical reasoning, independent judgement, ethical edge and spontaneous humour make him a man of many colours. His dedication to truth and non-violence, self-suffering, self-simplification drew their strength from Vedic Wisdom. He not only appreciated John Ruskin or Tolstoy or Thoreau but he lived them. His ideas on politics, economics, health, interfaith unity are known. His educational philosophy, however, needs closer attention. This book is a step in that direction.

For Gandhiji, end and goal of life was to promote truth and non-violence. In his life he promoted a climate congenial for others to live a life of truth and non-violence. Service to others, self-suffering, self-restraint, egolessness, fearlessness were the warp and woof of *satyagraha* and *sarvodaya.* He makes a distinction between better quality of life and higher quality of life. Better quality of life provides greater freedom to choose more earning, better food, house and clothes. Higher quality of life converge on self-restraint, self-suffering and self-control.

This second decade of the 21st century will lead us to more globalization, more explosive growth of information technologies, more competitive society, more violence, more inequality. If we want to enhance peace, non-violence, individual dignity, human rights and work for all, we ought to keep alive the spirit of Gandhian thought.

Except some honourable exception, the young in general are drifting away from thoughts and teachings of Mahatma Gandhi. Every effort must be done by the system and the individuals to help younger generation gain a wider vision of Indianness and a desire for promoting world peace and harmony. Knowledge about life and work of Mahatma Gandhi helps us in this venture.

This book is a thick description of Gandhiji views on education which he referred as his, **'Educational fads'** (Autobiography p. 185). His educational fads were based not on well designed educational principles and theory but on his own inner workings of ideas which were essentially ethical. He saw education as means to man-making which ought to have deep ethical potential. In criticizing education in 1919 and in 1937 he had expressed his shock wave of the then existing educational system which lacked teaching through mother tongue, value orientation, nationalism and dignity of labour. Gandhiji's educational views are embedded in Indian culture, which promote simplicity, hard work, non-violence, truthfulness, mutuality and social cohesion. He believed in multi level and multi dimensional thinking. To quote W.B. Yeats:

God guard me from the thoughts
Men think in mind alone
He that sings a lasting song
Thinks in the marrow bone.

Louis Fisher (2010 p. 216) makes a subtle observation that deserves our close attention. "India is fast forgetting the ideals of Gandhiji", he observed. Looking at the recent happenings in India, this observation cannot be negated or outright rejected. Scams, corruption, violence, inefficiency in work culture and self-exhibition traits of many of us point to the fact that Louis is not incorrect. Mohandas became Mahatma by understanding and living a life of self-control, self-discipline, self-service and self-effacement. Fisher further rightly observed, "Gandhiji was not only the property of India but of the whole world. He may die in India but remain alive in the world. In the end, he will remain alive both in India and the world".

To end, three notes:

(1) Repetitions have been built knowingly to make chapters self-contained.

(2) The term "man" is used in a generic sense and includes both genders.

(3) Examples cited are only illustrative not exhaustive.

(4) References as Autob means Gandhi M.K. 2004 i.e. An Autobiography : The Story of My Experiments with Truth.

E-250, Mayur Vihar-II
Delhi - 110091
Oct. 2nd, 2014

—Onkar Singh Dewal

Foreword

The freedom struggle of India continues to be studied, analyzed and interpreted globally for several of its unique and innovative features. Indian independence was a rare instance in human history when an individual fought against a mighty power only with the weapon of non-violence and won the war. The very strategy of non-violent struggle conceptualized and concretized by Mohandas Karamchand Gandhi not only succeeded in evicting the mighty British Empire from India but also became the leading light for freedom struggles of many countries. The man and his convictions, principles and practices are being studied with far greater endeavour and insight globally as the world aspires to get rid of violence, distrust and bigotry. An array of numerous luminaries; from Martin Luther King Jr. to Nelson Mandela; acknowledged that it were the principles postulated by Gandhi that inspired them in monumental struggles and achievements. To Mohandas Karamchand Gandhi, the "World was but one family"! Wherever and whenever people tired to establish superiority over others on the basis of diversities like the colour of skin, racial diversity or religions, the consequences were invariably disastrous. With the evolution of dynamic and responsive education systems, things began to change for the better. Slavery and apartheid are now history. Lack of education and ignorance inflicted innumerable miseries on nations and people. India had a very sound education system which was destroyed by the alien rulers. Mahatma Gandhi realized much earlier in his life that the root cause of all the miseries that India had suffered under the subjugation of the British was the planned, 'destruction of the Indian system of education' and, as a consequence of the same; the, 'delinking of Indians from their own culture and heritage. To him mere lifting of the alien yoke was not sufficient to put India on the path of progress unless India resurrected its own system of knowledge creation, generation, utilization and transfer to future generations, In a letter, he wrote on January 22, 1922 he puts things in a rather anguished perspective: "We should remember that immediately on the attainment of freedom, our people are not going to secure happiness.

As we become independent, all the defects of the system of elections, injustice, the tyranny of the richer classes as also the burden of running administration are bound to come upon us. People would begin to feel that during those days, there was more justice, there was better administration, there was peace, and there was honesty to a great extent among the administrators compared to the days after independence. The only benefit of independence, however, would be that we would get rid of slavery and the blot of insult resulting therefrom." In the same letter he goes onto suggest the solution: "But there is hope, if education spreads throughout the country. From that people would develop from their childhood qualities of pure conduct, God fearing, love. Swaraj would give us happiness only when we attain success in the task. Otherwise India would become the abode for grave injustice and tyranny of the rulers." Unfortunately, the policy-makers and implementers in education in the post-independence era ignored these futuristic and prophetic words of their mentor and now India suffers erosion of moral ethical and humanistic values to shocking levels. No one knew India better than Mahatma Gandhi and nowhere else in the freedom struggles against colonial powers; one finds so much emphasis on evolving a country-specific model of education as in India, solely because of Mahatma Gandhi.

'Pure conduct, fear of God and love', were the qualities he wanted to be developed right from the childhood. If education in Independent India had really incorporated these in the requisite measure, education would have prepared young men and women of unimpeachable character and commitment. It would have strengthened the pillars of social cohesion and religious amity. Instead, Indian education gradually discarded the very presence of religions in education in the name of secularity. One of the most brilliant minds of the freedom struggle C. Rajagopalachari wrote in the post-independence period: "Mass education…, which is to result not only in knowledge and mental preference of the Good but in capacity and readiness to work and suffer for it, cannot, as far as I see, be organized except on a religious base, religious in a broad sense". He thought that to treat religions as untouchable was one of the many unfortunate follies. India stands for righteous conduct and that accepts diversity and respects all faiths and religions on equal footing. This perception leads to spirituality at its best and the world respects India for the same. Who could be a better secularist than Gandhi? He always claimed that he was a Sanatan Hindu and everybody loved that. Why can Indian education not be based on this highest level of interpretation of religions and spirituality and move towards a value-based life for all?

When I open the book, "M.K. Gandhi: The Educationist Par Excellence", authored by Professor O.S. Dewal, I am delighted to find, and go through, second chapter on, 'Evolution of Consciousness'. The chapter encapsules the basic essence of educational foundations that have the potential to convert an individual from, 'A person to a personality'. This chapter makes a very strong point: No nation could afford to neglect the treasure of its own treasure and tradition of knowledge and wisdom. It has to be reinterpreted appropriately in the current and futuristic context. Every nation is passing through a moral crisis though its contours and elements may vary depending on various specific contexts. It has to develop its own models. Education in every country must be rooted to culture and committed to progress. This element comes out very prominently in this well researched, incisively documented and presented with emotion and sincerity which would be evident to every reader. This book presents before the reader a firm basis for formulating the education policy for the future. There can never be finality in the content and process of education as it is an organic dynamic entity. Mahatma Gandhi once wrote: “The real difficulty is that people have no idea of what education truly is. We assess the value of education in the same manner as we assess the value of land or of shares in the stock-exchange market. We want to provide only such education as would enable the student to earn more. We hardly give any thought to the improvement of the character of the educated”.

Prof. O.S. Dewal is one of the few veteran teacher educators who are respected for their scholarship and scholarly publications that are read with keen interest. He is living example of *“Yavadjivait Adhiyate Vipra:”* The manner in which he has related Indian tradition, the growth and life of Mahatma Gandhi and the evolution of his perceptions in education for India is indeed unique. He presents Gandhi Ji was a, ‘complete person’ and how a *Vaishnava* of Gandhi’s perception transcends all sectarian and religious boundaries. He calls himself a *Sanatan Hindu* and goes on to define it in a manner that would bring in every person of character, morals and principles within the fold, without impacting his religion and belief. This is real secularism that projects the best out of religion; in fact every religion; and paves the way for internalization of the principle of, ‘Universal unity of all human beings’. In the Sabarmati Ashram, Gandhiji made it compulsory to adhere to eleven vows none of which would impact adversely any person, sect, faith or religion. In Indian tradition, all the eleven of these have been respected, accepted and practiced for ages. Non-violence, truth, non-stealing, non-accumulation, physical labour, respect to all religions, fearlessness are the proud possessions of Indian family tradition. He added celibacy, not eating for pleasure and use of countrymade articles also to this list. Finally it is Truth and Non-violence that encompasses all of these. Essential objective was preparation of the, ‘complete man'. In the words of Swami Vivekananda, it was, “man making education”. And that was the objective that found the prominent place in his educational philosophy and practices of implementation.

Education policy and its implementation in India, he was convinced, would find it impossible to neglect the poor, ill-fed, deprived and exploited. He wanted every act and action to be examined a priory how far it would help the, 'last man in the line'! Post-independence policies have failed on this front. It can be achieved only if desires are to be renounced, necessities reduced to minimum and only needs are fulfilled, not for few but for all. To many, it may appear utopian in the times of unbridled materialistic pursuit. The fact, however, remains that there is no other way out that could create a peaceful, harmonious world that respects man-nature mutuality and gives dignity and humane life to everyone. This volume has very lucidly brought out what could be the, 'syllabus', for the young and old alike and could lead to value inculcation and internalization the lack of which engulfs the society under the debris of corruption, exploitation, tensions and turmoil. Published for the first time in the, Young India of October 22 1925, the Seven Social Sins, also indicated what a prophetic insight Gandhiji had for the, 'shape of things to come'. A critical appraisal, scrutiny and analysis of all these seven in the contemporary context could lead to healthy insights and; may be; certain ways and means to rectify the state of confusion, tension and uncertainty that prevails globally at present. *Politics without Principles* was the first one and everyone would agree to its capacity to inflict insurmountable damages to the system of governance. *Wealth without work*, attracts all and *Commerce without Morality* has become the order of the day. The glamour of Pleasure without Conscience combines with Commerce without Morality, and leads to *Religion without sacrifice* gets unprecedented acceptance. Violence and wanton exploitation of nature and its resources are an obvious consequence the application of, *Science without Humanity*. In totality, these seven sectors, if handled adequately by education in its content and process could transform human life for the better.

It is impossible to reject Gandhian philosophy of education. Education is supposed to lead every person towards 'right faith', right knowledge and right conduct. This is what education is supposed to achieve. And if it succeeds, this world would get rid of misery, poverty and sufferings of varied kinds. These can be achieved only after social evils are vanished by the educated and through the process of universalizing education. The description of Gandhi, his life and struggles and the assessment of his contributions during his lifetime has been aptly presented in this book. It further indicates that generations ahead shall continue to incisively analyze and study these for centuries ahead. They shall take inspiration from, What Albert Einstein had to say: "Generations to come will scarcely believe that such a man as this ever in flesh and blood, walked upon the earth". They would be amazed to read the concluding lines of the judgment delivered by the British Judge who convicted him on March 10; 1922 but also wrote the historic lines; "Even those who differ from you in politics look upon you as a man of noble and of saintly life". There are numerous instances that give the glimpse of the universal impact Mahatma Gandhi created through what he once said, "My life is my message".

Indian education system can no more ignore its responsibility towards the millions who have aspired for generations to lead a good, healthy and dignified life. On one side, India could rightly be proud of the recognition of its talent as evidenced by the presence of enterprising young Indians earning huge packages in NASA and Silicon Valley, but must also recognize the presence of millions of jobless young persons and another equally numerous set of those working on a pittance, solely due to lack of opportunities of skill orientation and job opportunities. To Gandhi simplification of life was the solution. But it did mean deprivation. It meant control/renunciation of desires, reduction of necessities and fulfillment of needs. Our education system prefers to swim with the tide, globalized world believes in accumulating as much as possible and that too in the shortest possible time. Why Indian educational planners have not the courage to find out what is best for India and Indians, remembering that it just cannot be a copy of an alien model but must have its roots deep in the soil of India. That would include India's culture, history, heritage and the knowledge tradition. This book authored by Professor Dewal is a concise synthesis of Gandhian philosophy and resulting practices in the specific context of education. His interpretations and articulation come directly from the heart. Those who have the privilege of working with him know, how he has engrossed himself in education endeavour for over six-decades following the Gandhian values in life and living. That he is emotionally attached to values and practices presented in this book become clear on several occasions. The narrative links ancient tradition in spirituality and quest and transfer of knowledge to the modern approach that primarily depends on advances in sciences and the support systems that have been provided by technology and particularly by the communication technology. Education is the key to human happiness. Gandhi has paved the path for one and all to march ahead on it. Professor Dewal provides an enriching opportunity to teacher educators, teachers and all those interested in the progress and development of Indian education a revealing opportunity that solutions are not difficult to assimilate once one internalizes faith in Gandhian philosophy and practices which harmonize faith, philosophy, spirituality, science and reveal the path for marching ahead to knowledge society.

—J.S. Rajput

Director, NCERT (1999-2004)

Chairperson; NCTE (1994-99)

January 05, 2014

Contents

Preface *7*

Foreword *13*

1. Prologue 23
2. Evolution of Consciousness 31
3. Mahatma: The Person 55
4. Education: An Extended View 81
5. Leave Schools and Colleges 107
6. Nai Taleem: Background and Concept 121
7. Seed Germinates and Withers 131
8. Paradigm for Re-engineering 141
9. Epilogue 149

References *155*

1

Prologue

We propose to start the *Prologue* with poetic expression by a *dingal* (Rajasthani) poet Thakur Nathu Singh Mahiyaria of Udaipur. He had composed *Gandhi Satak* (hundred *dohas*) describing various aspects of Gandhiji, his vision, his thoughts, his deeds and activities. The composition was greatly appreciated by eminent educationists and social-political leaders. Five couplets with English renderings are given here followed by explanations. English rendering are done by me, which are imperfect and I beg pardon of the readers. It lacks the charm of the *dingal* couplet that has music, imagination and creative expression.

- आजादी रखजे अमर आ मन प्रभू अभिलास।
  कर ज्योड्या विनती करे गांधी मोहन दास॥

  Mohan begs the Master of World's Kingdom
  Ever and eternal keep my India's freedom

(Mohandas Gandhi request the Almighty God with folded hands, 'Keep the freedom of India eternal and unending').

- आतम बल सो बल नहीं आतम बल अधभूत।
  जो जरमन सू जीतियो हार्‌यो गांधी हूत॥

  Soul force is Supreme, powerful and best
  Who won the Germans lost to Gandhi's zest

(The force of the Soul or the Spirit is matchless. It is indeed wonderful and surprising that the one who won the Germans got defeated by Gandhi).

- खग न लेतो हाथ में सेल न लेतो साथ।
  गांधी अनसन लेवतां लेतो फिरंग निसास॥

  Gandhi gripped never a sword or spear
  His fasts made British tremble with fear

(Gandhi never ever held in his hand neither a sword nor a spear. But undertaking self-suffering and undertaking fasts made the British fearful, disorganised and demoralised).

- गांधी चसमो राजरोघड्यो अनोखेघाट।
  तोने माछर दीखता लंदन वाला लाट॥

  Gandhi your spectacles shaped in shop unique
  Lords of London appeared mosquito and meek

(Gandhiji's spectacles were made and manufactured in some special shop. Because seeing through these spects the Viceroy from London was just seen as an ordinary person).

- बप पलटयो बावन हुवो, करतावर धर काज।
  गांधी पट न पलटियो, लेण गयो सुराज॥

  Lord of the World became dwarf for the cause
  Gandhi changed not his clothings for Swaraj

(The God wanted to chastises the wicked King Bali and thus became dwarf person and went to him and begged him some land, three steps in dimension. In two steps he covered the whole Universe and then killed Bali. Gandhi did not even change his dress when he met the King Emperor in 1931).

In these pages we will see the "*Guru*" aspect of Shri M.K. Gandhi. A Guru has three connotations; one who is great, who removes darkness and who has unique power of attraction. In ordinary parlance, the first meaning of the word comes with "*laghu*" and *guru* (small and big). In the second, "*gu*" means darkness and "ru" means removal or destruction of darkness. In the third sense, Guru means one who attracts others, have power of attraction, *gurutva sakti*. Gandhiji was great. He removed our ignorance when he said, "Who brought the English here?" "We". "Who are keeping the British here?" "We". "Only our brave and selfless and joint efforts can remove the British from India. If we get united, work boldly and selflessly, the British will cease to rule us." "No one can sit on our back if we stand erect", he said.

He had unique power of attraction. Look to the words of Pt. Jawaharlal Nehru: "His smile is delightful, his laughter infectious and he radiates light-heartedness. There is something childlike about him which is full of charm." Look to the words of Shri Moti Lal Nehru: "The man of poor physique had something of steel in him, something rock like which did not yield of physical powers. And inspite of his loin cloth and bare body, there was a royalty and Kingliness in him." Look to the words of Gopal Krishna Gokhale: "Gandhiji, without doubt, is made of the stuff of which heroes and martyrs are made. He has in himself the marvellous spiritual power to turn ordinary men into heroes and martyrs."

Gandhiji was an Acharya. A *sloka* (verse) beautifully describes Acharya; (a) one who studies all aspects of life in various spiritual literature; (b) one who critically examines all the aspects and selects the best; and (c) one who lives those principles and advises others to live according to those identified rules of life. The *sloka* is as follows:

अचिनेति हिशास्त्रार्थन, आचारे स्थापतस्युत।
स्वयं आचरतेयस्तु स आचार्य प्रचक्षते॥

Gandhiji indeed did all things. He (a) looked into different scriptures; (b) he identified the main behavioural implications; (c) he lived those principles in his life; and advised others to do so. Let us look at his critical expression. Agreeing with Lord Buddha, he said, reduce your wants, your necessities, your demands. He lived this principle. Look to his food and his dress. He found, "fear", the main cause of human misery. He advocated fearlessness. He lived the life of a fearless person. He read the Bible, the Koran, the Jain and *Sanatan* literature. He found that all religions have common root. They differ at the branch level. He recognized the truth in all religions and followed it throughout his life.

Human beings think and feel. Animals also think and feel. The only difference between human beings and animals and plants is that human being have the ability to evolve their consciousness. At one level we have animal consciousness, at another level we have man-consciousness. At another level we have *deva* consciousness. We move from animal or devil (आसुरी) to human (मानवीय) to Godly (देवत्व) consciousness. Gandhiji was a person whose consciousness was always in the process of evolution. His well-known quote that he will not wall his house, close the door and windows of his house but he will not leave his innate identity and cultural traditions show the Indian identity, openness to other cultures and an attitude of gradual evolution.

Gandhiji believed that we all are *amritya putra*. There are no high or low castes. Dignity of all individuals must be recognized. He called the untouchable as Harijan and worked throughout his life, to remove the concept of untouchability from the Hindu mind.

A Guru has to be, "complete man". A complete man is an *yukta* person, one who knows his end-point (or objective) and knows the process of reaching there; what the Gita (18.18) calls as process of knowing *jnana* ज्ञानं and the end goal *jneyam* ज्ञेयं. For Gandhiji the *jneyam* (ज्ञेयं) was the dignity of the individual, the autonomy of the individual and one's role in shaping one's future. The *jnana* (ज्ञान), the process to reach there was through truth and non-violence.

Gandhiji was a complete man; one who knew his goal and the process to reach there. The word, "complete man", is from *Learning to Be* (1972), a Unesco document chaired by Edger Faure. The term man here (and also in this book) is a generic term that connotes "a person". It does not exclude women. It includes them. The complete man has creative and critical mind, large and compassionate heart, abiding moral and ethical values. He improves himself and the society by his productive vision. Such a person always is in a process of progressive evolution by self-learning. For individual fulfillment and collective welfare the complete man integrates the physical, ethical aspects of life. He is, as they say, "Sagely within and kindly without". And Gandhiji was one such man who was in the process of constant evolution, *abhyudaya* (अभ्युदय).

We may see Gandhiji as a *yukta* person with the meaning as in the Gita. A *yukta* person is a person who is steadfast (कूटस्थ), who controls his senses विजितेन्द्रय and one who is saturated with rational and intuitive knowledge ज्ञान विज्ञान तृप्तात्मा (Gita 6.8). Such a person constantly performs his duty without expecting any gain for the self कर्म फलं त्यक्त्वा (5.12).

Indian scripture (*Atharva Veda; Brahmcharya Sukta*) gives, **five qualities of an excellent teacher**. A teacher must:

(i) Kill the negative traits of his students.
(ii) Must put-in special efforts to develop positive qualities.
(iii) Provide dynamism.
(iv) Provide strength to lead purposeful life.
(v) Inculcate qualities of calmness and tranquillity.

These five qualities are represented by words: (1) death *mrityu* (मृत्यु), (2) medicine *ausadha* (औशध), (3) air *varun* (वरूण), (4) milk *paya* (पय), and (5) moon *soma* (सोम).

In activities relating to *Satyagraha* (सत्याग्रह) in South Africa and India, Gandhiji tried to perform all the five stated functions. He killed in himself and his associates the spirit to harm and overpower others, provided medicines through his activities of *Satyagraha* and constructive programmes. By his individual behaviour he inculcated dynamism, cheerfulness and strength. Gandhiji, with severe self-discipline and self-control killed his negative thinking and undercurrents of untruth and violence. His favourite Gujarati song: "*Vaishnava jana….*" lists 20 chief traits of personality and he tried to live those (Iyer 2006 p. 63-64). A *Vaishnava* is a person who:

1. Is ever active in bringing relief to the distressed.
2. Takes no pride in doing.
3. Is respectful to all.
4. Speaks ill of none.
5. Is self-controlled in speech.
6. In action.
7. In thought.
8. Holds all in equal regard.

9. Has renounced desires.
10. Is loyal to one woman, his wife.
11. Is ever truthful.
12. Keeps the rule of non-stealing.
13. Is beyond the reach of *maya.*
14. Is, in consequence, free from all desire.
15. Is ever absorbed in repeating Rama's name.
16. And as a result has been sanctified.
17. Covets nothing.
18. Is free from guilt.
19. From the urge of desire.
20. From anger.

Another prayer Gandhiji was very fond of hearing and reciting was from John Henry Newman. It goes as:

Lead kindly Light among the encircling gloom
Lead Thou me on
The night is dark and I am far from home
Lead Thou me on
Keep Thou my feet I do not ask to see
The distant scene one step enough for me

Gandhiji was a unique time manager. In Indian Opinion of 25 March, 1905, under the title, "The Value of Stray Moments", (Iyer 2006 p. 204), Gandhiji writes that we waste stray time that lie between end of one task and beginning of another. If we add up stray moment they make no mean part of our life; not to make a proper use of them is to waste life itself.

On the importance of non-violence Gandhiji says that, "It is effective both in public and private life". But non-violence is impossible without complete self-effacement (Iyer 2006 p. 240).

Charles F. Andrews (1871-1940) a close associate of Rabindranath Tagore and Mahatma Gandhi, the only person to call Bapu by his first name "Mohan" has devoted a full chapter on The Background of Hinduism, in his book, *Mahatma Gandhi; His Life and Ideas*. There Gandhiji lists six points and calls himself *Sanatani Hindu* (*ibid.,* p. 8). We give below the gist:

- I believe in Veda and Upanishads, Avtars and rebirth.

- I believe in Varnashrama, dharma but not in its popular and crude form.

Caste system in India and the race prejudice in South Africa are very similar.

- I believe in cow protection.
- I do not disbelieve in idol worship.
- I implicitly believe no one truly knows the Scriptures who has not attained *Ahimsa, Satya*, Self-control and who has not renounced all possession of wealth.
- I believe in God, His oneness, in rebirth and salvation.

Gandhiji never believed in untouchability. He even said, "If untouchability is a part of Hinduism, I am not a Hindu". He objected to sacrifice of goats at the Kali temple. He criticized unhealthy conditions in temples. He was a teacher in the truest sense of the term. We must know about him more and know the unknown aspects of his life. His words were powerful, his deeds were more powerful, his silence was the most powerful. Gandhiji was an extraordinary teacher; a teacher *par excellence*.

"To believe in something and not to live it is dishonesty."
"Be the change you want to see in the world."
"The less I have, the more I am."
"Full effort is full victory."

□

2
Evolution of Consciousness

- *You have undertaken to secure freedom through the miracle, not of learning, but of character, secure it not by meeting the Government, sword against its shining sword but with peaceful spiritual effect... We want now to sow the seeds of freedom and afterwards will water the plant and rear it into a tree... I have given the mantra. I fulfilled the function of a rishi if a vanik's son can do so.*

  (Gandhiji's inaugural speech at the setting of Gujarat Vidyapeeth, 15 November 1920)
- *"It was not through books that one could impart training of the spirit.... Training of spirit was possible only through exercise of spirit. And exercise of spirit entirely depends on the life and character of the teacher" (Autobio p. 311).*

Plate 2.1

Through study of spiritual scriptures, experience and deep reflection, Gandhiji gained the highest level of consciousness. His life, after going to South Africa in 1893 started changing. The inner changes became distinctly visible when he finally returned to India in 1915. Some of the foundation principles on which he built his perspectives may be summarized as:

- At the root, all religions have a common core of the Truth. The Supreme Power, called by different names, rules all animate and inanimate objects.

Plate 2.1: (*Contd.*)

- Knowing the above point well, it is the duty of one and all to work hard to improve oneself, the society and the world.
- Work for good of all has to be executed with *nishkama bhava*, at the point of excellence, and with a cheerful temper.
- The above frame of mind demands adherence to Truth, non-violence, non-stealing, celibacy and non-accumulation. A life of sacrifice (*tyaga*) has its own reward.

Gandhiji's words from his Autobiography (p. 463) need be read and re-read to understand the inner working of his mind.

> "To see the universal and the all-pervading Spirit of Truth, face-to-face one must be able to love the meanest of creation as oneself. And a man who aspires that cannot afford to keep out of any field of life. That is why my devotion to Truth has drawn me into the field of politics. And I can say without slightest, hesitation, and yet in all humility that those who say that religion has nothing to do with politics do not know what religion means."

2.2 Evolution of Consciousness

Indian spiritual literature largely divide consciousness in two broad categories; lower and higher consciousness, the lower one focused to physical and materialistic side, the higher to the spiritual side, standing on the pillars of austerity, doing good to all, self-sacrificing, giving to others, sharing and caring. The Gita calls one that is physical, materialistic centred as *bhoga, aesvarya, prasaktanam* (2.44) भोग एश्वर्य प्रसक्तानां another is that of a *atmanvana* आत्मवान that is living life rooted to "Truth", living life beyond the three *gunas* निस्त्रेगुण्य living beyond dualities of pain or pleasure, loss or gain, defeat or victory, cold and warm, etc. [referred to in the Gita (2.45)] as *Nirdvando*. Gandhiji lived the life of *bhog* and ashvarya and then saw its hollowness and uselessness and then lived the life of *atmavana*. We may say, he lived from 1869 to 1893, an average life and from 1893 to 1948, a life of higher consciousness, although even in his life from 1869 to 1893 he had elements of higher consciousness. He was never a victim of laziness and lethargy, he always believed in the truth, non-violence and adhered to three vows he had taken.

From 1893 onwards he indeed lived a saintly life of the highest order, "God laid the foundations of my life in South Africa and sowed the seeds of the fight for national self-respect (Autobio. p. 130). In 1906, he took the vow of leading a celibate life. He renounced all gifts given to him from 1896 to 1901 and constituted a trust before going to India in 1901 (Autobio. p. 204). At the lowest level of consciousness one is engrossed in *tamsic* and *rajas* activities that are centered in काम, क्रोध, लोभ (which the Gita refers as doors of hell) one who is rooted in ignorance, one who has arrogance, pride, self-high estimation दम्भ, दर्भ, मान व मद. A person of higher consciousness has full control over his senses. The Gita observes that one who controls his senses is *sthitprajna* वशे हि यस्ये इन्द्रियाणि तस्य प्रज्ञा प्रतिष्ठिता (2.61) one who is careful about what to eat, when to eat and how to eat. Mahatma Gandhi strictly followed Gita's wisdom on food. Our food shapes our personality अन्नात् भवति, भूतानि. Gandhiji believed in, "We are what we eat". Gandhiji used to say, *yatha aana tatha manna*. Our food shapes our mind and thoughts. The guiding principle is eat less *laghavashi* and take appropriate food, appropriate to constitution."

A person of higher consciousness is always cheerful and does his duty mindfully, carefully and without expecting any gains for his well being. The main educational import that we receive from the life of Gandhiji is that a thoughtful person must constantly evolve himself to higher level of consciousness. That is the goal of life, purpose of life, aim of life.

We now look at his eleven vows that he decided in 1915 and kept them throughout his life. These vows give us an opportunity to see deep into Gandhiji's consciousness.

2.3 Eleven Vows

Gandhiji founded Phoenix Farm in 1904 and Tolstoy Farm in 1910 in South Africa, where it was agreed upon, by all inmates, to lead a simple life, dedicated to truth, service to others and non-violence. When Gandhiji came to India in 1915 and when he decided to settle in *Sabarmati Ashram*, he made it compulsory for inmates that they will adhere to eleven moral and social principles. Those were:

- Non-violence — *Ahimsa* — अहिंसा
- Truth — *Satya* — सत्य
- Non-stealing — *Astyaya* — अस्तेय
- Celibacy — *Brahmacharya* — ब्रह्मचर्य
- Non-accumulation — *Aparigraha* — अपरिग्रह
- Physical Labour — *Sareer Srama* — शरीर श्रम
- Fearlessness — *Abhaya* — अभय
- Not eating to please palate — *Aswada* — अस्वाद
- Respect to all Religions — *Sarva Dharma Samabhave* — स्वधर्म स्वभाव
- Use of country made articles — Swadeshi — स्वदेशी
- No faith in non-touchability — *Sparsha Bhavana* — स्पर्श भावना

When Gandhiji went to the YMCA, Madras on 16 February, 1915, students requested him to speak on the Banaras University incident. On this suggestion, he observed that it was an incident that need not be stressed much. He said that he would speak on Ashram Vows and would like students to understand those vows and, if possible, live those vows. **He strongly advocated for *Sparsha bhavana*, strongly rejected the notion of untouchability.** He explained the principle of truth in thought, speech and action. He also said, “In this Ashram, we make it a rule that we must say what we mean, regardless of consequences” (Iyer p. 284).

> *"As I look back upon the twenty year of the vow, I am filled with pleasure and wonderment. The more or less successful practice of self-control have been going on since 1901. But the freedom and joy that came to me after taking the vow had never been experienced before 1906."*
>
> *Autob. p. 192*

While explaining the meaning of *Truth*, Gandhiji said, "It is much more than not telling the untruth. It is, being truthful in thought and feeling. In a way God is Truth. *Ahimsa*, he said, means non-killing but it also includes not offending anybody, not harbouring any uncharitable thought even against the enemy. The vow of **celibacy or brahmacharya** is avoiding sensuous and sex experiences which are contrary to *dharma*." The Gita (7.10) says, "I am sensuous pleasure which is not inconsistent to dharma." धर्माविरुद्ध भूतेषु कामोऽस्मि भरतर्षभ । Gandhiji led very pure life as a student in London (November, 1888-June, 1891). He started leading a celibate life after 1901 and finally took the vow of celibacy in 1906.

Vow of **non-stealing**, which is referred by Gandhiji as "non-thieving" (Iyer p. 287). We may extend this concept a little further. As a teacher if I do not do full preparation for day's teaching, I am thieving and stealing something. If a teacher goes late to school, he is also thieving and stealing.

Vow of **non-possession** refers to not accumulating more than what is needed. We have only a few wants or needs but we have more of necessities and a massive amount of desires. We ought to curtail drastically and keep only to our bare wants and needs. Lord Buddha and Lord Mahavir both stressed the need to reduce wants and needs.

The above five vow appear in *Yogasutra* of Patanjali as *Yama* and in Jainism as *Pancha Mahavrata* पंच महाव्रत, Gandhiji added six more that had social significance. Those vows relate to control of palate, physical labour, fearlessness, respect to all religions, use of country made articles and faith in touchability. Vow of the **control of palate** helps a person to control his animal passions. Gandhiji was totally against exciting stimulating foods that can be put under, "gourmet category". The concept of *chappan bhoga*

छप्पन भोग delicacies shows that we are slaves to the palate and not the master.

His next vow relate to undertaking **physical** labour. The trend of avoiding physical work was clear in 1915. People would put in mental labour (doctors, engineers, lawyers, teachers) but would avoid physical and bodily labour. Gandhiji made it a point to put in physical labour. Even a respected guest of the Ashram would have to undertake physical work after the 3rd day of his or her stay in Ashram. When Gandhiji and Sri Sankar Lal Bunkar were arrested on Friday, the 10th of March, 1922 (10.30 p.m.) and were produced before the District and Session Judge, Brumfield, on 18th March, 1922, Gandhiji told the court that he was a weaver and an agriculturist (Fisher 2010, p. 67).

The vow of **fearlessness** has its root in the Gita (16.1). When Sri Krishna explains the qualities of a divine-oriented person, he puts fearlessness as the first quality as *devi sampada.* We find an overt expression in Hind Swaraj as well as in, Quit India Movement.

Gandhiji thought that fearlessness is essential for the growth of other noble qualities (Andrews 2006, p. 292). Fearlessness includes no fear of death, or disease, or injury or dispossessions and loss of one's dear and near ones. The seeker of truth and non-violence overcomes all types of fears. All fears disappear when one is not afraid to die. Strength lies in absence of fear. "That nation is great which rests its head upon death as its pillow."

> *"You need not consider that you have not hurt our feelings by your conduct. We are not expressing our sentiments either through base selfishness or fear but because it is our duty now to speak out boldly. We consider your schools and law courts to be useless."*
>
> *(Hind Swaraj p. 88)*

Gandhiji believed that **all religions must be respected**. Root of all religions is the same; they differ with respect to rituals and processes which are just the branches of the tree. All regions stand for love and helping the needy; all religions advocate eliminating one's ego, arrogance and pride; all religions demand non-crookedness (*aarjavam*) in behaviour. Thus, Gandhiji respected all religions. During his prayer meeting quotes from all well-known religions were recited. Gandhiji undertook a fast of 21 days for Hindu-Muslim Unity from 18th September, 1924 from the house of Maulana Mohammad Ali. On completing 21 days, he asked Andrews to sing a Christian prayer, Imam Sahib to recite Sura from Holy Kurana and Sri Vinoba Bhave to recite *slokas* from *Upanishads*. Dr. Ansari offered him a glass of orange juice (Fisher p. 71-72).

Gandhiji's concept of **Swadeshi** was an evolving concept. His swadeshi vow quoted in his letter of 8 April 1919 (Iyer p. 363):

> *"With God as my witness, I solemnly declare that from today I shall confine myself for my personal requirement, to the use of cloth manufactured in India from Indian cotton, silk or wool and I shall altogether abstain from using foreign cloth, and I shall destroy all foreign cloth in my possession."*

In his letter he beseeched every Hindu, Mussulman, Sikh, Parsi, Christian and Jew to take the *Swadeshi* Vow and ask others also to do likewise. He also said that if we can do this much for our country, we are not born in it in vain. On another occasion, Gandhiji made an appeal to merchants to stop all importation of foreign cloth. His concept of Swadeshi, is most vivid and daring, when he says, "I tell Rajendra Babu everyday that it is better for us to starve than to import even a single grain of food from outside" (Iyer p. 374).

2.4 Thoughts Speak

Verbal expression, known as (*bakhari*) is audible. But many times our inaudible thoughts also speak. Gandhiji, in one of his correspondence wrote, "Our thoughts speak". One reader could not understand. In the letter to Gandhiji (October 16, 1947 published in Harijan on 26 October 1947) he wanted to know how thoughts communicate. To him Gandhiji's reply was as given as in the box:

This reply needs to be understood properly. It speaks of Gandhiji's modesty and truthfulness. It is visible. But without using

> *"There is a stage in life when a man does not need even to proclaim his thoughts, much less to show them by outward action. Mere thoughts act. They attain that power... I must confess that I am far from that state."*
>
> *(Iyer p. 44)*

technical terms of shastras he is referring to four types of *vani; para* (परा); *pashyanti* (पश्यन्ति); *madhyama* (मध्यमा) and *bakhari* (बेखरी). It is believed that those who are fully established in God (बह्मनिष्ठ) can communicate in *para* and *pashyanti vani*. This communication is non-verbal. In *madhyama* and *bakhari* language is used for communication. In *madhyama* words are used in brief, pithy axioms or sutra form. In *bakhari*, thoughts are communicated through words and are audible.

Words are effective means to communicate factual information. But when communicating emotions and deeper meanings, language becomes an ineffective tool of communication. Only most competent persons can make their language communicate emotions. What Gandhiji says in his letter is that some people develop power to speak in *para* and *pashyanti vani* when their unspoken thoughts reach the listener.

As thoughts speaks, so also our body language and our micro facial expression. Gandhiji used many times body language, and micro facial expression to communicate his inner feelings. We have an excellent example. In the Gita (2.9) when Arjuna finally says that he will not fight (न योत्स्य), Shri Krishna offers a smileful look प्रहसन्निव. This facial reaction contains the gist of the Gita. The smiling face of Shri Krishna communicates:

- Arjuna is under elusion and advances hollow argument without deep reflection.
- Under the spell of emotions Arjuna thinks that it is good to abjure war; for it is a sinful act to kill ones relatives and respectable ones.
- I will soon help him to see the hollowness of his argument and focus his mind on his "duty", which must not be forgotten.

- When logic and arguments will sink in his mind, Arjuna will come out of his present despondency.

2.5 Increasing Dislike for Medicines

Gandhiji used to have three square meals daily with as many delicacies as he could have. He often had headaches. He then dropped breakfast; after a few days headaches entirely disappeared (Autob. p. 248). With diet control and use of earth and water treatment one can control many ills. He says, "999 cases out of a thousand can be brought round by means of well regulated diet, water and earth treatment." He also said that one who runs to doctor for every ailment and swallow drugs becomes a slave of his body instead of being its master and ceases to be a man (Autob. p. 249). He further says (Autob. p. 251) "Who lives in the fear of God must restrain in diet both as to quantity and quality it is as essential as restraint in thought and speech".

2.6 The Gita: His Infallible Teacher

Rise in levels of consciousness also includes our faith and respect to scriptures. In a letter to Gulzarilal Nanda dated May 28, 1927 Gandhiji writes, "At the present moment though I am reading many things, the Bhagvad Gita is becoming more and more the only infallible guide, the only dictionary of reference in which I see the sorrows, all the troubles, all the trials arranged in the alphabetical order with exquisite solutions" (Iyer p. 172). Gandhiji started reading the Bhagvad Gita when he was in England. The Gita stresses doing one's duty attentively, cheerfully and without caring for self-interest.

Gandhiji had faith in Indian spiritual scriptures, but his was not a blind faith. He used to evaluate statements and traditions also rationalistically. He also says that many things in our *purans* like marrying girls at a young age need not to be accepted now. Similarly he advocates that *yajna* is not animal sacrifice, it is selfless action, it does not involve sacrifice of animals. He is convinced that aim of religion is self-transformation, self-upliftment, self-empowerment and social reform. The teachings of the Gita include no malice, fearlessness, no ill-feeling, no anger, *nirvaira, abhaya, adyesha, akrodha* (निर्वैर, अभय, अद्वेष, अक्रोधद्ध). These are the pillars of non-violence and promote global peace and social cohesion. The Gita teaches to do our obligatory duty. Gandhiji said "The Gita is my mother" (Harijan October 3, 1936). The Gita teaches to tolerate pleasure and pain with equanimity. Those who are steadfast in their wisdom tolerate pain of senses समदु:ख सुखं धीरं (2.15). Those who are lost in self-glorification and lost in sensuous pleasure भौगेष्वर्य प्रसक्तानां (2.44) do not have the right wisdom, steadfast buddhi.

When Gandhiji was in London for his Bar at Law studies, he came in contact with two English people who were reading the English translation of the Gita by Sir Edwin Arnold — the *Song Celestial*. They invited Gandhiji to read the original. He was sad to tell them the truth that he neither knows Sanskrit nor has read the Gita. In London, he read the Bible and compared the Surmon on the Mount with the teachings of the Gita.

In South Africa, Gandhiji's fascination of reading increased and he decided to remember verses by heart. He invented a unique method. In the morning hours he used to take thirty-five minutes for toothbrush and bath. On the wall of the bathroom he, "Stuck slips of paper on which were written the Gita verses". He could look at them for memorization. He committed to memory thirteen chapters (Autob., p. 243).

Gandhiji's rising level of consciousness can also be seen by readings his views on *varnashram dharma*. He considered untouchability a curse in Hinduism. *Verna* system is a sin. It is a distortion brought in later on. Andrews (p. 120) quotes Gandhiji, "If untouchability belongs to Hinduism, I am not a Hindu". The Gita categorically says सम: सर्वेषु भुतेषु (18.54). With correspondence with different people he stressed the need to remember all the 700 *slokas* of the Gita by heart. He found great solace in reading the Gita which has a deep message for our lives. It helps us to dedicate ourselves to our duty.

Gandhiji respected all religions and faiths and considered them true and genuine. He himself studied different religious literature including the Bible, the Koran and Tolstoy's The Kingdom of God is within you. In a letter dated November 1, 1945 (Iyer p. 159-60), Gandhiji writes, "The root of all religions is one and it is pure and all of them have sprung from the same source. Hence all are equal."

There are wise sayings in Indian scripture that point out Vedas, *smrities* and *rishi muni* differ. There are conflicting views on dharma also. The sure guide to our action and activities are the acts of the wise. The great people's life and work must be followed and imitated.

Srutih Vibhinna smrtasyo bhinnah
Na ako muniryasy varchanh pramanum
Dharmam tatvam nihitam guhayan
Mahajano yena gatoh sa pantha
श्रुतिः विभिन्ना स्मृतितस्य भिन्ना न को मुनिर्यस्य वचः प्रमाणाम्
धर्माम् तत्वम् निहितं गुहायान् महाजनोयने गतः स पंथा

Our scriptures say that we must entertain, receive and accept good ideas and noble thoughts from all over the world. आनो भद्रा क्रतवोयन्तु विश्वत्. *In Young India, Gandhiji wrote, "I don't want my house to be walled in all sides and my windows to be stuffed. I want the cultures of all lands to be blown about my house as freely as possible".*

On the unity in the diversity of cultures and religion, even in recent times, Ramakrishna Paramhansa said: *Yata mata tata path* यता मत तथा पथ. As many views as many religions Path (the path). The direction one takes must be guided by three elements: scriptures, reasoning and personal experience; what *Samskara* calls a *sruti, yukti, swanubhuti* श्रुति, युक्ति and स्वानूभूति. No religion demands blind faith. All religions demand faith based on reason. And faith is to be lived and experienced. We see this reasoning in Gandhiji's consciousness. **And that makes him a teacher extraordinary.**

Another aspect that needs to be seen is, there are rituals where religions differ but there are core teachings on which all religions agree. Persons with higher consciousness separates the core and the non-essentials. All religions believe that we must help and give something to the needy. We must be kind and large-hearted. We must remember sincerely the creator as often as we can. We must be trustful, kind and compassionate to others. When we want to explore unity in diversity, our approach combines:

- Rational and intuitive aspects.
- This worldly welfare as well as other-worldliness.
- Individual as well as social well-being.
- Humanistic as well as spiritual orientation.
- Passion to do one's duty zestfully and cheerfully and maintaining disinterestedness.

2.7 The Educationist Speaks

Over the years Gandhiji evolved as an educationist. We have devoted separate chapters on this theme but here we give as illustrations, his other thoughts as an educationist, that include; life-long learning need of civility and fearlessness, home education, abjuring wealth and humility.

Importance of educating expecting mothers: Over the year Gandhiji realized that the first five years of the child are the most important years of learning. It is wrong to think that child has nothing to learn during the first five years of its life. He further adds, "The education of the child begins with conception. The physical and mental states of the parents, at the moment of conception, are reproduced in the baby. Then during the period of pregnancy it continues to be affected by the mother's moods, desires and temperaments, as also by her way of life" (Autob. p. 188). Gandhiji had two sons born in South Africa. He decided to know all about childbirth and early upbringing. He closely studied *Ma-ne-Shikhman* by Dr. Thribhuvan Das. He nursed both children according to instructions he read in the book.

Importance of civility and fearlessness: The Kheda Satyagraha started because the crop, due to famine got destroyed. Only one-fourth (four *anna*) crop was available. As such the farmers under revenue rules, were exempted from paying revenue money. Farmers (*patidars*) made several petitions and prayers to the commissioner but of no avail. Gandhiji then started Satyagraha with Sardar Vallabhbhai, Sankarlal Banker, Srimati Ansuyabehn and others. Patidars refused to pay the revenue assessment and were ready for all consequences including legal action and forfeiting their land. The government realized the situation and agreed to the non-collection of land revenue.

In this context Gandhiji mentions (Autob. p. 401-2) that he wanted *patidars to realize the duty of combining civility with fearlessness.* But Gandhiji realized that people *"Had less fully realized the lesson of civility than he had expected". He said, "Experience has taught me that civility is the most difficult part of satyagraha. Civility does not here mean the mere outward gentleness of speech cultivated for the occasion but an inborn gentleness and desire to do the opponent good."*

• **Home Education:** Gandhiji believed that "home education", is better than "school education". Home education includes inculcating qualities of discipline, liberty and self-respect (Autob. p. 186). In 1920, Gandhiji called out the youths from schools and colleges as they were receiving miseducation. It is better to live with self-respect than to receive education that lacked nationalism, patriotism and love for liberty. Leave schools and colleges, the call of Gandhiji in 1920s was to seek liberty, discipline and self-respect.

One of the greatest hallmark of *Sanatana* (or Hindu) *Dharma* is to see the multiplicity in the unity सर्वे खल इदम् ब्रह्म. This world or the whole of the cosmos has a purpose, a goal. It has its *rta* ऋत. It is not mindless. Home education must include this also. Cosmos has its laws and moves according to them. It works within its set boundary. All religions at the root, have uniform principles. Remaining faithful to one's religion, we must respect all religions.

• **Abjuring Wealth and Family Attachment:** Gandhiji decided to lead a life of *vanaprastha*, a life of chastity (*brahmacharya*) in 1906; although he had thought about it in 1900 or so. In 1906, he took this decision after consulting his wife. He offered his services to the Natal Government at the time of Zuhu Rebellion. He shifted his wife and children to Phoenix Farm. It was during this period that he took the decision to relinquish wealth and family attachment. He writes, "If I wanted to devote myself to the service of my community in this manner, I must relinquish the desire for children and wealth" (Autob. p. 190).

• **Humility:** A way of life: In the Amritsar Congress Session the King's announcement on new references on India was the point on which Gandhiji had a difference of opinion. He was for it and Lokamanya Tilak was against. But he did not wish to disagree with seasoned great leaders like Lokamanya Tilak and Deshbandhu. He thus pleaded with Malviyaji to absent himself from the Congress for the rest of the session. This request shows two aspects of greatness of Gandhiji. One, to give expression to one's inner voice, and two, to respect elders and great national leaders. His request to absent himself from the rest of the Congress session was in response to meet these two objectives.

In Indian Opinion (25 December 1909), Gandhiji translated, "Tolstoy's letter to a Hindoo", in Gujarati and added a preface to it. There he asserts that we are our own slaves, not of the British. We invite suffering on ourselves through our own faults. Slavery consists of submitting to an unjust order not in suffering kicks. The British cannot remain if we do not want them. We can drive them out not by fire arms but by our soul force (Iyer p. 73-75).

In a letter to Wybergh, Member of the Legislative Assembly, Transvaal (Iyer p. 88-92) (appeared in Indian Opinion, 21 May 1910), Gandhiji agreed to many criticisms raised by Mr. Wybergh about his views in the booklet *Hind Swaraj*. He accepted criticism cheerfully. We are reminded of a quote by Robert Frost, "Education is the ability to listen to almost anything without losing your temper and self-confidence". Gandhiji was a living example. Gandhiji believed in his inner conscience and was his own master. He sought the Kingdom of God from within.

At another occasion (Iyer p. 86-88), when he was asked to speak on East and West on 13 October 1909, he said that modern civilization worshipped body not the spirit. Modern facilities, railways and medicine, add to our bodily comfort but do not raise our moral standards. Only self-simplification, self-suffering and self-purification can add to the glory of the spirit.

Gandhiji came to India in 1901 but had to return to South Africa in 1902 as Lord Chamberlain was visiting. He reached Durban and drafted the Memorial. He also started practicing in Transvaal Supreme Court and set up office in Johannesburg. His interest in self-simplification and religious conversations gradually increased. The Gita became his infallible guide. The terms अपरिग्रह and संभाव gripped his imagination. Trusting his belief that one should be only a trustee of what one has, he allowed his insurance policy (in India) to lapse and started using his earning for the good of the community rather than sending to his brother (Autob. p. 244-5). The Indian Opinion got started in 1904. And he started a life of self-imposed poverty, renouncing his legal income which was £3,000 yearly.

Gandhiji gave a new interpretation to the term *aparigraha*, which, in common sense, is non-accumulation of material things. One can extend this idea to include non-accumulation of intellectual wealth as well. Always consider oneself as a "beginner". If one feels proud about his learning, he may not learn many new things. But if one feels that one is only a beginner, one will have capacity to learn many new things. In *Gita Mata* (p. 332), Gandhiji writes, "When the pot is full even God cannot add anything into it. One must stand before God empty-handed." Will Durand said many years later, "Education is a growing knowledge of our ignorance".

2.8 Seeing the Person Through His Words

Before we go to the next chapter, it is good to see Gandhiji through his own words. We have selected a few of his sayings that bring out his mindset or his educationist aspect. **Whether it is education or economics or politics, spiritualism is his foundation stone.**

- "When I landed at Durban in January 1897, I had three children with me … Where was I to educate them? … I could have sent them to Schools for European Children but only as a matter of favour … There were schools established by Christian Missions but I was not prepared to send my children there as I did not like the education imparted in these schools… I am of the opinion that if I had insisted on their being educated somehow at public schools, they would have been deprived of their training that can be had only at the school of experience or from constant contact with parents."

(Autob. p. 184)

- When Gandhiji was removed from his seat in the train at Maritzburg, he began to think of his duty, "Should I fight for my rights or go back to India… It would be cowardice to run back to India… I should try to root out the disease."

(Autob. p. 104)

- It has always been a mystery to me how men can feel themselves honoured by the humiliation of their fellow beings.

(Autob. p. 143)

- All other pleasures and possessions pale into nothingness before service which is rendered in a spirit of joy.

(Autob. p. 161)

- Sir Pherozeshah seemed to me like the Himalaya, the Lokamanya like the ocean. But Gokhale was the Ganges.

(Autob. p. 164)

- My life is based on disciplinary resolutions… I pledged myself never, whilst in India, to take more than five articles in twenty-four hours and never to eat after dark.

(Autob. p. 359)

- During the farewell party by Abdulla Sheth, Gandhi, read, incidentally, that Indians will not have right to elect members of the Netal Legislative Assembly. He made up his mind to stay on. He then writes, "Thus God laid the foundation of my life in South Africa and sowed the seed of the fight for national self-respect".

(Autob. p. 130)

- "Our present education system does not help us control

our senses and does not enable us to do our duty. Character building must have the first place in it and that is primary education."

(Hind Swaraj p. 78-79)

- "Indian civilization is the best and that the European is a nine days wonder."

(Hind Swaraj p. 89)

- "We have hither to said nothing because we have been cowed down but you need not consider that you have not hurt our feelings by your conduct. We are not expressing our sentiments either through base selfishness or fear but because it is our duty now to speak out boldly."

(Hind Swaraj p. 88)

- "Nine hundred and ninety nine cases out of a thousand can be brought round by means of well regulated diet, water and earth treatment and similar household remedies. He, who runs to doctor, vaidya or *hakim*, for every little ailment, not only curtails his life but, by becoming slave of his body, instead of remaining its master, loses self-control and ceases to be a man."

(Autob. p. 249)

- "I do not know who is a Gandhian. Gandhism is a meaningless word for me. An ism follows the propounder of a system. I am not one, hence I cannot be the cause for any ism. If an ism is built, it will not endure, and if it does, it will not be Gandhism."

(Iyer p. 62)

- "I have always held that it is only when one sees one's own mistakes with a convex lens and does just the reverse in case of others that one is able to arrive at a just relative estimate of the two. I further believe that a scrupulous and conscientious observation of this rule is necessary for one who wants to be a *Satyagrahi*."

(Autob. p. 432)

- "Be the change you want to see in the World."

(Covey 2009 p. 153)

- The difference between what we can do and what we could do would suffice to solve most of the world's problem.
(Covey 2009 p. 311)
- "Sweet are the fruits of patience. Deeds like seeds take their own time to fructify."
(Hind Swaraj)
- "In the dictionary of a Satyagrahi, there is no such thing as defeat. To him, the very pursuit of his battle is its own reward."
(Iyer 2010, p. 129)
- "*Satyagraha* was born in South Africa in 1908. A Gujarati speaking gentleman substituted the word satyagraha (for passive resistance that in Hindi is *Nishkriya Pratirodha*). And it was adjudged the best."
(Iyer 2010, p. 308)
- "A man's reforming zeal ought not to make him exceed his limits. [The Gita advises to undertake activities mindful of our limitations and strengths (अनवेश्य च पौरूषम् 18.25)]."
(Autob. p. 247)
- "I am painfully conscious of my imperfections and there lies all the strength that I possess, because it is a rare thing for a man to know his own limitations."
Andrews (2006 p. 280)
- "I think the word "saint", should be ruled out… it is too sacred a word to be lightly applied to anybody much less to one like myself… The politician in me has never dominated a single decision of mine."
(Iyer p. 44-46)
- "Vow is a promise made by one to oneself. Vows are good for character building. We should never doubt the necessity of vows for purpose of self-purification."
(Iyer p. 200)
- "I have undertaken to reform a single person and that is my ownself. And I realize how difficult it is to reform him."
(Iyer p. 206)

- "My language is aphoristic, it lacks precision. It is, therefore, open to several interpretations."

  (Terchek 2000 p. 1)
- "The Great faiths of the world are so many branches of the tree, each distinct from the other, though having the same source."

  (Harijan, January 18, 1939)
- "Each living faith must have within itself the power of rejuvenation, if it is to live."

  (Harijan, September 28, 1935)
- "I must confess that I do not draw a sharp line or any distinction between economics and ethics. Economics that hurt the moral being of an individual or a nation are immoral."

  (Young India, October 13, 1921)
- (In a letter dated, April 17, 1918 Gandhiji listed 15 instructions for volunteers of Kheda Satyagraha). We list a few below:
  - They must abide by truth.
  - There is no room for rancour, satyagrahi should not utter any harsh word about anyone.
  - Rudeness has no place in satyagraha. Perfect courtesy must be shown.
  - When in villages, volunteers should demand the fewest services from the village-folk. They should avoid using vehicle. They should reach a place on foot.
  - If they can, volunteers must teach the village children.
  - They must insist on being served the simplest food.

  (Iyer p. 314-15)
- We must speak out without fear the plain truth. We must make our lives meaningful by realizing our insignificance and thus become meek as a lamb and strong as a lion by contemplating *chaitanya* that is with us.
- Lord Willington, the Governor of Bomaby said that he feels greatly disappointed when he meets Indians, for they do not express what is in their minds but only what will

be agreeable to him, so he never knows the real position. (Iyer p. 103)

- "A nation that is desirous of securing home rule cannot afford to despise its ancestors. We will become useless if we lack respect for our elders. Mr. A.O. Hume and W. Wedderburn, founded, Indian National Congress to spread discontent among Indians. Reform always must be preceded by the discontent. It was the respected Dadabhai who taught us that the English had sucked our life-blood." (Hind Swaraj p. 20)
- "You cannot breed peace out of non-peace. The attempt is like gathering grapes of thorns or figs of thistles." (Harijan, 4 June 1938)
- "The Working Committee of Congress.... have come to the conclusion that they are unable to go to the full length with Gandhiji. But they recognize that he should be free to pursue his great ideal in his own way, and therefore absolve him from responsibility for the programme and activities which the Congress has to pursue. The difference between Gandhiji's approval and that of the Working Committee must be understood and must not lead people to think that there is a break between him and the Congress. The Congress of the past 20 years is his creation and child and nothing can break this bond. I am sure his guidance and wise counsel will always be available to the Congress." Jawahar Lal Nehru, 23 June 1940 (Iyer p. 252)

Gandhiji seriously challenges the economic idea that higher consumption leads to more production, and more production leads to better national economy. Gandhiji's thinking is based on cosmological ideology rather than on narrow ideology of high and more production. He advocates for voluntary limitation of consumption for the good of all. He wanted labour-intensive (not capital intensive) development built on local skills and resources.

2.9 Gandhiji's Lifeline (1869-1948)

- 1869 2nd October–Birth in Porbandar

- 1883 Marriage with Kasturba
- 1885 Death of father
- 1887 Passed Matriculation Examination
- 1888 Birth of Hiralal
- 1888 4 September leaves for England to study Law
- 1891 10 June — Passes Bar at Law
- 1891 12 June — Leave for India
- 1891 7 July — Reaches Bombay and receives news of his mother's death
- 1892 Starts legal practice in Rajkot and Bombay
- 1892 Birth of Manilal
- 1893 Leave for South Africa
- 1897 May — Birth of Ramdas
- 1900 22 May — Birth of Devadas
- 1915 9 January — Arrives in Bombay
- 1915 20 May — Establishes Satyagraha (Sabarmati Ashram)
- 1917 31 August — Meets Mahadev Desai
- 1924 12 January — Operated for appendicitis
- 1933 26 July — Leaves Sabarmati Ashram and establishes in Wardha
- 1942 15 August — Mahadev Desai dies
- 1944 22 February — Kasturba Gandhi dies
- 1948 30 January — Martyrdom, 5.10 p.m. Last words uttered 'Hey Ram'.

At the end let me quote Dr. APJ Abdul Kalam (2003, p. 88-99) that spiritualism has always been the foundation stone of India's priceless heritage. Gandhiji lived it in his life.

> *"Our Spiritual Wisdom has been our strength. We survived the onslaughts of invaders and the numbing effects of colonialism. We have also learnt to adjust to the rifts and divisions in our society. But in the process of all the adjustment we also lowered our aims and expectations. We must regain our broad outlook and draw upon our heritage and wisdom to enrich our lives."*
>
> *Dr. Abdul Kalam*

Plate 2.2

2.9 Some Indian Leaders with whom Gandhiji was closely associated and date of their death

- 1915 19 February — Death of G.K. Gokhale
- 1917 30 June — Death of Dadabhai Naoroji
- 1920 1st August — Death of Lokmanya Tilak
- 1925 20 June — Death of Deshbandhu Chittaranjan Das
- 1926 Martyrdom of Swami Shraddhanand
- 1931 4 January — Death of Mohammed Ali in England
- 1933 20 September — Death of Annie Besant
- 1933 22 September — Death of Vitthalbhai Patel
- 1936 10 May — Death of Dr. Ansari
- 1941 7 August — Death of R.N. Tagore
- 1946 12 November — Death of Madan Mohan Malviya

□

3

Mahatma: The Person

- *"The Mahatma has won the heart of India with his love; for that we have all acknowledged his sovereignty. He has given us a vision of shakti of Truth for that our gratitude to him is unbounded. We read about Truth in books, 'We talk about it: but it is indeed a red-letter day, when we see it face-to-face'. Rare is the moment, in many a long year when such good fortune happens".*

  (Rabindranath Tagore)

  (Bhattacharya 2001, p. 68)

- *"The path of self-purification is hard and steep. To attain to perfect purity one has to become absolutely passion free in thought, speech and action; to rise above the opposing currents of love and hatred, attachment and repulsion. I know that I have not in me as yet the triple purity, in spite of constant ceaseless striving for it. That is why the world's praise fails to move me indeed, it very often stings me."*

  M.K. Gandhi

  (Autob. p. 464)

3.1 Lifeline: A Quick Glance

Gandhiji was born in Porbander on 2nd October 1869. His father, Karamchand Gandhi and his grandfather Uttam Chand Gandhi were Prime Minister in Porbander. He joined Rajkot school and passed matriculation exam in 1887. Before this he was married to Kasturba in 1883. On 4th September 1887 he was sent to England for Bar at Law. There he passed his London Matriculation Exam and passed Bar at Law. Called to bar on the 10th June 1891, enrolled in the high court on 11 June and sailed for India on 12 June 1891. In Rajkot he could not establish his legal practice. He left for South Africa to help Dada Abdulla & Co. in April 1893.

When Gandhiji was born, Swami Dayanand Saraswati was 45 years old, Rabindranath Tagore 9 years old, Vivekanand was 6 years old. The English Empire was 11 years old and English education system, which started with Lord T.B. Macaulay's Minutes on 2 February 1835, was 34 years old. The comparative historicity will help us gain a comprehensive picture of social and political trends in the country.

Gandhiji was in South Africa (S.A.) from 1893 to 1914, with few short duration visits to India.

- April 1893 — Sails to S.A. as the Legal Adviser to Dada Abdulla & Co. and sailed back to India on 5 June 1896. He was in India from June to November 1896.
- 30 November 1896 — Sails back to S.A. Arrives in Durban on 13 January 1897.
- 18 October 1901 — Sails with family to India and returns to S.A. again on 20 November 1902.
- 18 July 1914 — Sails for London *en route* to India and arrives in Bombay on 9 January 1915.

To gain a broad understanding and an overview of Gandhiji's life, it is better to put his activities under broad time periods like Earlier Years (1869-1888), Visit to England for study (1888-1893), Life in South Africa (1893-1915), Life in India I (1915-1920), and India II (1920-1948). Under each period we will put only important happenings. This exercise may appear meaningless and superficial to those who are devoted students of Gandhiji but for the new generation, it may be a useful input as they know very little about Mahatmaji. Studies conducted on students recently have shown that they mix and mingle relationship between Mahatma Gandhi and Rajiv Gandhi.

Earlier Years (1869-1888)

When Gandhiji was born on 2nd October 1869, the British Empire was 11 years old. After the first war of independence (1857) the British Crown took India under its direct control in 1858. At that time the capital of India was in Calcutta. Gandhiji was married to Kasturba (age 13) in 1883 when he was 14 years of age. He passed his Matric Exam in 1887, and joined a College in Bhavnagar but couldn't fit in the academic system and thus withdrew from college studies. On the recommendation of his well-wisher and with full love of his elder brother he was sent to London to study Bar at Law.

Study in London (1888-1891)

When Gandhiji was 18 years old, he set sail for England from Bombay on 4th September 1888. In England he strictly kept three vows given to him by his mother. But he did spent money on playing an Englishman. Purchase of an evening suit, taking dancing lessons, violin, western music and French are some of the examples. But the awareness that he is not to live in England for ever made him give up all.

In the second year of his stay in London he came in contact with theosophist and on their advise read The Song Celestial and The Light of Asia by Edwin Arnold. He also read The Bible. He specially liked the sermon on the Mount. He also visited France. Finally completed his Bar at Law on 10 June 1891 and sailed to India on 12th June 1891.

Legal Practice (1891-1893)

Gandhiji started his practice from Bombay but could not succeed. Applied for the post of an English Teacher for an hour daily for ₹ 75/- per month but was not selected. He set up office in Rajkot. There also he could not succeed. Meanwhile he received an offer to go to South Africa with first class return fare and a sum of £105 for legal assistance for not more than a year. He sailed in April 1893 with, 'full zest'.

In South Africa (1893-1914)

With two brief visits to India in 1896 and 1901, Gandhiji remained in South Africa for nearly 21 years and from Mohandas Karamchand Gandhi became the Mahatma. It was here that his **thought line** changes significantly. He decided to live for the good of others for their dignity and autonomy. As poetically visualized by Robert Frost, he took less travelled path:

Two roads diverged in a wood,
And I took the one less travelled by,
And that has made all the difference.

Gradually he, more and more, embraced self-sacrifice, love for others, self-purification, reduction of wants and cultivation of soul force. He discovered that passive resistance was the answer. In September 1906 in Old Empire Theatre in Johannesburg, Indians under his guidance accepted Soul Force or Passive Resistance to undo the Asiatic Registration Act. Indians agreed that violence in any form was to be eschewed. Self-suffering was the way to secure lasting reform. Nearly 2,500 Indian suffered imprisonment in Transvaal. Gandhiji received a letter from Tolstoy in 1909 wherein he wrote, "Your activity in Transvaal as it seems to us at the end of the world is the most essential work, the most important of all the work now being done in the world."

Gandhiji's first son Harilal was born in 1888 before he left for England for study. His second son Manilal was born in 1892 before he left for South Africa. His third son Ramdas and the fourth son Devadas were born in South Africa in 1897 and 1900 respectively. Gandhiji celibacy practices started in 1900, culminated in 1906.

In England (1888-1891) he faithfully kept the three vows given to his mother — Developed interest in vegetarianism. It was in England that he developed interest in religion, which became deeper and deeper in South Africa. He resolved to work against the black law of apartheid. Read Tolstoy, Thoreau, Ruskin, The Bible. Reading of these books led him to read more on Hinduism. He writes, "I should read more religious books and acquaint myself with all the principal religions". **This one line of thought entitles us to call him educationist par excellence.**

Education is zero without character and source of character formation resides in religions. In South Africa, when he went second time in January 1897, he had three options to education three children who were with him; to send these children to schools for European children. He rejected this option. To send them to school established by Christian Missions. He rejected. To send them back to India for education. He rejected this idea as he felt that young children should not be separated from their parents.

Gandhiji kept an English governess for a month or so. He himself took the responsibility to teach them. He accepts that these experiments were inadequate but he could teach them the simplicity and the spirit of service. He considers, "My object in discussing the subject here is that a student of the history of civilization may have some measure of the difference between disciplined home education and school education and also of the effect produced on children through changes introduced by parents in their own lives."

Later on Gandhiji did two big experiments, one in 1920 and another in 1937. He, in 1920, gave a call to students to reject government schools and come out of citadels of slavery. These will be discussed in later sections.

With a few breaks, he lived in South Africa from 1893 to 1914. During his early years in South Africa he saw heart-rending discrimination between the white and the coloured people. The black and the brown were treated most inhumanly. He was himself a target on many occasions. He was thrown out of the first class compartment of the train, he was not given hotel accommodation as he was a coolie. And the barber will not cut his hair as he was brown. He inwardly decided that he will oppose this inhuman discrimination. And he did.

It was in South Africa where he started Natal Indian Congress, in 1894. It organized fierce campaign against Tax of £3 (which was originally of £25). His first experience of jail was in 1908 when he led 2500 India against 'Asiatic Registration Act' that did not recognize Indian marriages. Ultimately Government of General

Smuts agreed to the demands. And the Indian Relief Bill was passed. While fighting his war of passive resistance, he declared that he would march on 1st January 1914 with a group of satyagrahis. But at that time the white employees of Railway went on strike. He stopped his marched saying, "A satyagrahi's code of working is not to destroy or hurt the opponent". On 30th June General Smuts agreed to Gandhiji's demands.

> *Hind Swaraj was written in 1908 during my return voyage from London to South Africa in answer to the Indian School of Violence and its prototype in South Africa.*
> *(M.K. Gandhi 1938 p. 15)*

In 1914, Gandhiji received Gokhale's instructions to return to India. He sailed for England and then to India. Gandhi who left South Africa in July 1914 was a totally different person from the young lawyer who had landed in Durban in 1893.

In India (1915-1919)

Gandhiji came to India in the beginning of 1915. He went to Shantiniketan where the Phoenix boys were staying. And then to Poona to meet Prof. Gokhale. In February 1915, he was again in Shantiniketan when he knew about the death of G.K. Gokhale (on 19 February 1915). He spoke on 20th February on the work and services of Gokhale before Shantiniketan students.

Activities during this period relate to eradication of custom barrier between British India and Kathiawar State. He asked people (in 1915) to be ready to go to jail and offer *satyagraha*. Gandhiji had a talk with Lord Chelmsford and he agreed to remove the custom barrier. The second event related to prevention of indentured Indian labour being recruited for British Colonies. Deputation of ladies met Viceroy Lord Chelmsford and finally decided May 31, 1917, as the date from which the indentured labour should be stopped.

Gandhiji had gone to Lucknow in 1916 for the Congress session. There on the insistence of one agriculturist Raj Kumar Shukla, he visited Champaran for providing relief to Indigo planters. The people of Champaran maintained peace and order along with their leaders in thought, speech and action. In this campaign he met Acharya Kriplani and Dr. Rajendra Prasad. The authorities served Gandhiji a summon to leave Champaran which he refused to do. So Gandhiji's trial began in the Magistrate's Court. But the case was withdrawn and Gandhiji started his inquiry into the allegations made by the Champaran farmers. Later on the Lt. Governor of Bihar constituted a Committee which recommended abolition of *tinkathia* system.

The fourth struggle was that of mill-hands against their owners of Ahmedabad. Although most of the mill-owners were Gandhiji's friends and well-wishers but he found the cause of mill labourers, just and he advised them to go on strike, keeping in view four conditions:

- Never to resort to violence.
- Never to molest and criticize black legs or those who differ.
- Never to depend on other's mercy.
- Remain firm and earn bread by other honest means.

It went for many days (21). But after two weeks there was an atmosphere of despondency, despair and enthusiasm dwindled. As Gandhiji writes, "The strikers began to totter". Then an inner voice came and he declared, "Till a settlement is reached I will not touch any food". After three days the mill owners gave in and a settlement was reached.

In India (1919-1948)

On the instructions of Gokhale, Gandhiji didn't do anything for one year. He extensively travelled and saw India what it was. He set up his Ashram at Ahmedabad, visited Rangoon, and Servants of India Society, Poona, understood the cause of the problems of indentured labour and got it stopped before July 31, 1917, visited Champaran and brought relief to Champaran indigo farmers, helped the Ahmedabad Mill workers and got them better payments, supported the cause of Khera district farmers and brought them relief. He agitated against Rowlatt bill and started non-cooperation movement. He protested against Jallianwala Bagh's inhuman massacre. He asked people to non-cooperate with the government and made a nationwide call for boycott of schools, courts, jobs, honours and foreign cloth. In September 1921, he renounced clothing except homespun loincloth (*dhoti*) and a shawl.

Gandhiji in 1917 came in touch with a lady Gangabehn Majumdar. Gandhiji asked her to search for the spinning wheel for manufacturing of Khadi and to identify weavers to weave the yarn. Soon Ashram Khadi gained a name. Gandhiji further mentions (Autob. p. 451-54) his choice for Khadi *dhoti* of 45 inch width. He was then impatient for the exclusive adoption of Khadi. He writes (p. 454), "My cloth was still of Indian Mill cloth. The coarse Khadi manufactured in the Ashram at Vijapur was only 30 inches in width. I gave notice to Gangabehn that unless she provided me with a Khadi *dhoti* of 45 inch width within a month, I would do with coarse short Khadi *dhoti*. The ultimatum came upon her as a shock. But she proved equal to the demand made upon her."

Gandhiji undertook fast unto death in 1932 against separate electorates for the untouchables. He said, it is an attempt to make untouchability last forever. Rabindranath Tagore sent a telegram (19.9.1932), approving of his act.

"It is worth sacrificing precious life for the sake of India's unity and social integrity. Though we cannot anticipate what effect it may have upon our rulers, who may not understand its immense importance for our people, we feel certain that the supreme appeal of such self-offering to the conscience of our own countrymen will not be in vain..... Our sorrowing hearts will follow your sublime penance with reverence and love" (Bhattacharya 2001 p. 133).

Gandhiji's call **"Quit India"**, came in 1942. In-between he devoted himself for the removal of untouchability, Hindu-Muslim unity and village upliftment through cottage industries.

3.2 Self-Suffering for Social Ills

To understand gradual evolution of Gandhiji's consciousness, it is good to recall two instances when Gandhiji undertook self-penance for the wrong acts of other people. At the Tolstoy Farm, he was informed about the moral fall of two of the inmates of the

Farm. His reaction was unique and most unconventional. He felt that two persons who did undesired activities were certainly responsible for their wrong act. But he, as their leader, was indirectly responsible for their act. Thus he took upon himself double penance (Autob. p. 314), a fast for seven days and a vow to have only one meal a day for a period of four months and half. This act made double impact. All people realized not to repeat sinful acts. This act also made interpersonal relationships more genuine and strong.

Another event relates to the strike of the Ahmedabad Textile Mills Workers. They were demanding higher wages and the mill-owners were not agreeing to that. Gandhiji pledged his full support to the workers. As days passed he noticed some weakness in the determination of mill workers. He called the leaders and said, "Till the settlement is reached I will not touch food". The sacrifice on the part of Gandhiji and this penance made the mill-owners agree to workers demand.

> *The book is a several condemnation of modern civilization. It was written in 1908. My conviction is deeper today than ever. I feel that if India will discard "Modern civilization", she can only gain by doing so.*
>
> *(Hind Swaraj 1938 p. 15)*

It is true that Gandhiji severely criticized western civilization as it introduced machines and relegated the human beings to the margin. It had killed their souls. Although living in the Western Civilization Dadabhai Naoroji, whom Gandhiji met in London in 1888 greatly impressed him. He was bold enough to tell the British their rule in India was **UnBritish**. (*He wrote; Poverty and UnBritish Rule in India*). Gandhiji writes, "I myself and many others like me have learnt the lessons of regularity, single-minded patriotism, simplicity, austerity and ceaseless work from this venerable man", (Iyer p. 77).

Besides truth and non-violence Gandhiji believed in self-simplification and self-suffering. He would often resort to fasting. We have quoted two examples above which had unique reasons. In the second case Gandhiji undertook the fast to keep up the moral strength of the labour. In the first instance he took up the fast as he felt that as a father, he had his own responsibility in the downfall of inmates of Tolstoy Farm.

We may also record two more cases of his fasts which had special reason. In 1924, he took up the fast for 21 days for the cause of Hindu-Muslim Unity. With his will power and implicit faith in cause of the fast (Hindu-Muslim Unity), he survived without food for 21 days. On the last day he was offered a glass of orange juice by Dr. Ansari.

In 1942, on 14 July, Congress Working Committee, passed the resolution that colonial rule must end immediately in India, failing which Congress will launch non-cooperation movement under Mahatma Gandhi. The decision was to be operationalised soon after 8th August 1942. On the night of 8th August 1942, Gandhiji asked members to feel free from this very moment, Fisher writes (p. 148), "Feel that you are not under the Colonial rule". Thus Gandhiji implicitly taught; *not the circumstances but we are the master of circumstances.*

On the 9th August all senior leaders including Gandhiji were arrested. Lord Linlithgow blamed Gandhiji for mass unrest and mass violence that took place after 9th August. Gandhiji strongly opposed this point. He took 21 days fast. Gandhiji wrote to the Viceroy on 31 December 1942 that he has decided to sacrifice himself for the untrue allegation. As the Viceroy did not withdraw his allegation, Gandhiji started his fast on 11 February 1943. On 2nd March 1943, Kasturba Gandhi helped him to break the fast.

3.3 Teachers of Gandhiji

It is often said that those who want to move up in spiritual life must have a *"guru"*. But Gandhiji was an exception to this rule. He did not have any *"guru"*. And he had many. It is said that Dattatriya, son of Atri (father) and Anusuya (mother) had 24 *gurus*. Great Rishi Dattatriya had multiple teachers and learnt his lesson from each one of them. It is said that he learnt from the sun, moon, air, elephant, snake, spider and many more. This applies to Gandhiji also. He had no *Guru* and had many *Gurus*. Here we may mention five names; Rajchandra (or Raychandra) and Gopal Krishna

Gokhale with whom he had direct contacts. He established indirect contacts, through books, with Ruskin, Thoreau and Tolstoy. In Raychandra, Gandhiji found a person of moral earnestness. He was his *guru* in his moments of spiritual crisis. With him Gandhiji learnt one thing, **"Infinite striving after perfection is one's right. It is its own reward"**.

The second Indian *guru* was Gopal Krishna Gokhale. Gandhiji calls him his political *Guru*. He was impressed by his simple living, his devotion to the Motherland and his pure motives. In his words (Hind Swaraj, p. 19), "Professor Gokhale embraced poverty", in order to prepare the nation. He was greatly impressed by Gokhale's role in improving education.

Gandhiji's indirect gurus were Ruskin, Thoreau and Tolstoy. Gandhiji was not a voracious reader. But whatever he read, he read it mindfully and picked up the key message to live in life. He read Henry Thoreau's essay, *On Civil Disobedience*. Thoreau said, "To be right was more honourable than to be law abiding". Thoreau was against US policy of his times that condoned slavery. Gandhiji internalized the message and lived it throughout his life. In his letter of reply to Tagore (Young India 1st June 1921), he asserted that non-cooperation is not a doctrine of exclusiveness, narrowness and negation, (Bhattacharya 2001, p. 67). "In my humble opinion, rejection is as much an ideal as the acceptance of a thing. It is necessary to reject untruth as it is to accept truth.... Non-cooperation with evil is as much a duty as cooperation with good."

Gandhiji read John Ruskin's (1819-1900) *Unto the Last* and felt that the book created a magic spell on him. He read the book in 1904 in Johannesburg-Durban train. When the train reached Durban he mentally made a vow to renounce material possession and live his life according to the ideals of *aprigraha* अपरिग्रह. He also drew three conclusions from the book (Autob. p. 275), as given in the following box:

- The good of an individual is contained in the good of all.
- The lawyer's work has the same value as the barber's.
- A life of labour is life worthliving.

In this Autobiography (p. 275) he writes, "I arose with the dawn, ready to reduce these principles to practice". Phoenix Farm got started in 1904. In 1906, he took the vow of *Brahmacharya*. In the same year he launched the *Satyagraha.*

Gandhiji's another teacher was Tolstoy (1828-1910). Tolstoy advised non-violent means to resist injustice. Earlier Lord Christ said, "One must not resist evil by violence. Resisting evil by non-violent means is the only way open". Gandhiji in 1910, sent a copy of *Hind Swaraj* to Tolstoy. Tolstoy praised passive resistance of Gandhiji. Tolstoy Farm was established in 1910 on 1,100 acres provided by Harman Kallenbach.

According to Gandhiji, Western Civilization has:

- Pronounced individualism.
- Excessive consumerism.
- Self-exhibition.
- Decrease concern for social, cultural and spiritual values.

3.4 Mahatma: Seen Through Many Lenses

As people differ, so also their perceptions and judgement differ. Many people honestly believe that what they think, feel and perceive is right. Gandhiji was seen as "martyr", by Gokhale who closely observed him in 1912 in South Africa. He said, **"Gandhi is without doubt made of the stuff of which heroes and martyrs are made. He has in himself the marvellous spiritual power to turn ordinary men into heroes and martyrs"** (Nanda 1958, p. 83). In contrast to the above judgement on Gandhiji, we see Winston Churchill's judgement. When Viceroy Lord Irwin invited Gandhiji to discuss Home Rule matters, Churchill said, "The nauseating and humiliating spectacle of this one time Inner Temple lawyer, now seditious *fakir* striding, half-naked, up the steps of the Viceroys palace, there to negotiate and parley on equal terms with the representative of the King Emperor".

Authors of, **Freedom at Midnight** (p. 102) mentions that to Jinnah Gandhiji was a, 'cunning fox' and a Hindu rivalist. They also mention (p. 184) that in one July afternoon (1947) the man who had spent so many years in British jails walked into Viceroy's study room. There he asked Mountbatten to accept Congress's invitation to become the first Governor-General of the nation. The authors further write, "Mountbatten was overwhelmed". "We have jailed him. We have humiliated him. We have scorned him, we have ignored him, and he still has the greatness of the spirit to do this".

In his Autobiography Jawaharlal Nehru (1989 p. 129-30) sees Gandhiji through his lens. He writes, "After a brief political estrangement in the middle of 1924, the old relation between my father and Gandhiji were resumed and they grew even more cordial. However, much they differed from one another, each had the warmest regard and respect for the other. Father has given a glimpse into his mind in a brief foreword he contributed to a booklet called, *The Thought Current* containing selections from Gandhiji's writings."

Sri Moti Lal Nehru writes: "I have heard of saints and superman but have never had the pleasure of meeting them and must confess to a feeling of skepticism about their real existence. I believe in men and things manly. *The Thought Current*, emanated from a man and are things manly. They are illustrative of two great attributes of human nature, faith and strength".

Sri Motilal Nehru admired the strength of spirit of Gandhiji. *"This man of poor physique had something of steel in him, something rock like which did not yield to physical powers. And in spite of his unimpressive features, his loin cloth and bare body there was a royalty and a kingliness in him which compelled a willing obeisance from others".* Sri Moti Lal Nehru sums up his Foreword to, *The Thought Current* as: "The humble and lowly figure standing erect on a firm foothold of faith unshakable and strength unconquerable continues to send out to his countrymen his message of sacrifice and suffering for the motherland".

We have on the other hand Lord Willingdon's views about Gandhiji, "We found him slippery. To deal with a saint and a *bania* is very trying". Similarly Lord Linlithgow said, "He was world's most successful hung bug". Churchill called Gandhi and Nehru as paper tigers. Churchill and one-eyed soldier Lord Wavell considered him, "An irrelevant old fool". However, Albert Einstein on Gandhiji's death said, **"Generations to come will scarcely believe that such a man as this ever in flesh and blood, walked upon the earth."**

On 10th March 1922, the judge, while delivering the judgement said (Andrews 2006 p. 218), "The law is no respecter of persons. Nonetheless it will be impossible to ignore the fact that you are in a different category from persons I have ever tried.... It will be impossible to ignore the fact that in the eyes of millions of your countrymen you are a great patriot and a great leader. **Even those who differ from you in politics look upon you as a man of noble and of saintly life".**

Lord Readings had many meetings with Gandhiji. Subsequently he wrote a letter to his son. He writes, "He has nothing astonishing about his bearing but when he talks he gives a different impression. He is straightforward and speaks good English. He understands well the depth of meaning of words he uses. He is fearless and frank" (Fisher 2010 p. 67).

Louis Fisher (2010 p. 42) writes what an Oxford Professor, Prof. Gilbert Muir wrote about Gandhiji. "Be careful when you have to interact with this man. He is a person who cares nothing about pleasures and facilities, nor of his praise. He is dedicated to work which he considers truthful and purposeful. People can win his body anytime but, he never allows anyone to touch his soul". Jawahar Lal Nehru in his flowery language has described the coming of Gandhiji:

> *"We seemed to be helpless in the grip of some all powerful monster; our limbs were paralysed, our minds dead..... what could we do? How could we pull India out of this quagmire of poverty and dejection which sucked her in.... And then came Gandhi. He was like a powerful current of fresh air that made us stretch ourselves and take deep breaths, like a beam of light that pierced the darkness and removed the scales from our eyes like a whirlwind that upset many things but most of all the working of people's minds".*

In his Autobiography Nehru (1989 p. 515), also writes, "People who do not know Gandhiji personally and have only read his writings are apt to think that he is a priestly type long-faced and killjoy type. He is the very opposite. His smile is delightful, his laughter infectious and he radiates light-heartedness. There is something childlike about him which is full of charm. When he enters a room he brings a breath of fresh air with him which lightens the atmosphere".

At another place Nehru (1989 p. 516) writes, "He listens with greatest patience and attention to people who make new suggestions but behind his courteous interest one has the impression that one is addressing a closed door. He is so firmly anchored to some ideas that everything else seems unimportant". The moderates used to call him, "muddle-headed person". He would change his views if he finds them coinciding with the truth, Gandhiji used to act according to his, "inner voice". He had faith in his, "inner voice" and will act according to that. General Smuts jailed him and Gandhiji on his release presented the General a pair of shoes.

I am not worthy to stand in his shoes.
(General Smuts)

It is difficult to make a concluding statement on how others saw Gandhiji. His life, as he said, was his message. He was larger than his life. His deeds, as Rabindranath Tagore said, "Were more powerful than his words". "He was not made of the common clay", as Nehru said. His address to the nation on 30 January 1948 deserves close attention.

> *"Friends and Comrades, the light has gone out of our lives and there is darkness.... Our beloved leader Bapu, as we called him, the Father of the Nation, is no more. Perhaps I am wrong to say that. Nevertheless we will not see him again as we have seen him for these many years. The light that has illuminated this country for these many, many year will illuminate this country for many more years, and a thousand years later that light will still be seen in this country and the world will see it and it will give solace to innumerable hearts..."*

Again let us repeat what Tagore said about Gandhiji:

> *"The Mahatma has won the hearts of India with his love for*

that we all acknowledge his sovereignty. He has given us a vision of shakti or Truth for that our gratitude to him us unbounded. We read about Truth in books, we talk about it, but it is indeed a red-letter day when we see it face-to-face. Rare is the moment, in many a long year when such good fortune happens."

Tagore also said (in his letter of 6 February 1934), "Mahatma is one person who has done most to raise the people up from the slough to despondency and self-abasement to which they have fallen through centuries of servitude". Lord Mountbatten equated Gandhiji not with Roosevelt or Churchill but with Christ and Buddha.

We need to reflect deeply to see what was that spirit of Gandhiji that made him rock-like and steely. We quote below words of Gandhiji that transformed him from a mortal being to Mahatma. It relates to 1893 when he was thrown out of the train while travelling from Maritzburg (Capital of Natal). It was here he thought; whether it was good to go back to India or to go to Pretoria without minding the insult and then to return to India or to stay and fight this apartheid and racial segregation.

"I began to think of my duty. Should I fight for my right or go back to India... It would be cowardice to run back to India without fulfilling my obligation. The hardship to which I was subjected was superficial – only a symptom of the deep disease of colour prejudice. I should try to root out the disease and suffer hardship in the process" (Autob. p. 104).

When Gandhiji was at the Sasoon Hospital, Poona, after his operation of Appendicitis, he asked Charles F. Andrews to undertake the editorship of *Young India*. In one of the editorial Charles wrote:

"When all the buildings have crumbled into dust the name of Mahatma Gandhi will still be taught by mothers to their little children as one of the greatest of India's saviours" (Andrews p. 288).

3.5 Mahatma: Through his Own Lens

Gandhiji had faith in spiritual scriptures. He also had deep faith in reasoning and reflection. If he, after careful reasoning, took a stand he adhered to the stand come what may. Commitment to his inner voice was the chief trait of his personality.

Andrews (2006 p. 71) records observation of a visitor, "Truth and sincerely in every line of his face seem to demand the same in return. One should never be artificial with such a man for his keen vision penetrates all our wrappings".

We find Gandhiji often looking at himself in a joyful and informal way. He often laughed on himself. In the "Introduction to his Experiments with Truth" (pp xii-xv) he says that his life is being guided by religion which is morality, "The essence of religion is morality". His experiments with truth relate to non-violence, celibacy and truth. Truth for him is God. The truth which Gandhiji understands is truth of thought, of words and deed. In this scheme of things, ego has no place.

Another conviction he shares with readers is whatever is possible for him is also possible even for a child. The seeker after truth must be humbler than the dust. In his autobiography he acquaints the reader with all his faults and follies. In his charming simplicity he said, "I have nothing new to teach the world. Truth and non-violence are as old as hills". Andrews (2006 p. 280) records what Gandhiji once said, "I am painfully conscious of every imperfection and there lies the strength I possess because it is a rare thing for a person to know his limitations".

Kasturba was ill. Gandhiji advised her to abstain from taking salt and pulses. She was surprised. She remarked how anyone can drop taking salt and pulse. On this Gandhiji said, "Well, why not. I hereby will not take salt and pulses for one year." Kasturba followed him. Gandhiji writes, "And I gained the reputation of a quack".

On an occasion Gandhiji reacted to the word "Gandhism" (Iyer p. 62). We repeat that again here, "I do not know who is a Gandhian. Gandhism is a meaningless word for me. An ism follows the propounder of a system. I am not one, hence I can't be the cause for any ism". If an "ism" is built, it will not endure, and if it endures it will not be Gandhism.

3.6 Networking With Others

If we look at Gandhiji and his relationship with Winston Churchill, Tagore, Mrs. Sarojini Naidu, Gokhale, Tilak, Moti Lal Nehru, Madan Mohan Malviya and other leaders of early 20th century, we will see that each had his individual identity. We start with Churchill.

Winston Churchill was totally against India's independence. His position was very rigid. He called Nehru and Gandhi as paper tigers and called Clement Attlee a modest man with much to be modest about. When Churchill held his first meeting with Franklin Roosevelt to frame Atlantic Charter, he made it clear that India was not to fall under its provisions. When Gandhiji took 21 day fast from Aga Khan Palace, Gandhiji wrote to Lord Linlithgow, "I propose to crucify myself for the wrong allegation framed against me". Churchill observed, "If Gandhi wanted to starve himself to death, he was free to go ahead and do so". Churchill's inner voice always compelled him to say, "I have not become His Majesty's First Minister to preside over the dissolution of the British Empire".

When Gandhiji on 17 February 1931 went up the Viceroy's House to discuss matters with Viceroy Irwin, Churchill called Gandhiji, "half-naked fakir". To that observation Gandhiji's calm reply was "I want to become fully naked fakir."

Rabindra Nath Tagore and Gandhiji were two great Indians marked by their independent individuality and differences. If we see about them closely and critically, we will learn how mutual respect can live along with sharp differences and divergent perspectives. Great souls have rare virtue of seeing good in others yet maintain their own individuality.

The first meeting of **Mrs. Sarojini Naidu** with Gandhiji was in London in 1914. She describes her first meeting (Bandyopadhyay 1994 p. 25-26), "My first meeting with Mahatma Gandhi took place in London on the eve of the great European War of 1914. He had arrived fresh from his triumphs in South Africa. I went wandering about in search of his lodging in an obscure part of Kensington and climbed the steep steps of an old unfashionable house to find an open door framing a living picture of the little man with a shaven head eating a messy meal of squashed tomatoes and olive oil out of a wooden prison bowl".

I burst instinctively into laughter at the amusing and unexpected vision of a famous leader whose name has already become a household word in our country. He lifted his eyes and laughed back at me saying, "Ah, you must be Madame Naidu! Who else dare to be so irrelevant. Come in and share my meal". "No thanks", I replied. "What an abominable meal it is".

Along with Gandhiji she worked for Hindu-Muslim Unity. In 1919, with the passing of the Rowlatt Act, discontentment grew and Gandhiji offered Satyagraha. Hartal was observed on 6th April 1919. In Sabarmati Gandhiji called a conference of some devoted workers and Madame Naidu was one of them. On that occasion, she said (Bandyopadhyaya 1994, p. 28), "Satyagraha movement has kindled its fire in the temple of Ashram where Mahatma Gandhi is the high priest or guru. To speak the truth was good but to live the truth was better".

When the great trial of Mahatma Gandhi took place on 10th March 1922, Mrs. Naidu was in the court room. She writes in *Bombay Chronicle* (March 1922), "A convict and criminal in the eyes of the law, nevertheless people rose in the act of spontaneous homage when Mahatma Gandhi entered.... A frail, indomitable figure in a coarse and scanty loincloth.... and looking around to all who had come, he said", "This is like a family gathering and not a law court".

Mrs. Naidu took active part and associated herself with Gandhiji's movement against Salt Law in 1930. She was arrested and sent to jail. When Gandhiji picked up the Salt, Sarojini Naidu greeted the act with **"Hail deliverer"**.

When Gandhi went to East Bengal in 1946, she wrote from Shantiniketan, "Beloved Pilgrim setting out on pilgrimage of love and hope. I have no fear for you... only faith in Your mission."

Gandhiji's expression **"Himalayan miscalculation"**, was on the realization of his mistake, and his boldness to accept his mistake is an indication of intellectual and moral honesty. He launched *Satyagraha* on the assumption that people will be non-violent during non-cooperation movement. But people indulged in looting, violence and torture. This made him withdraw his non-cooperation movement which was seen as big mistake by people even very close to him, Pt. Jawaharlal Nehru. Many years later Nelson Mandela said, "Glory lies not in never falling but in rising everytime we fall". Truth has many coats likes an onion. Swami Vivekananda observed that we move from truth to truth and not from error to truth. Err and err but less and less.

Paramhansa Yoganand (1890-1952) has a chapter in the book, **Autobiography of a Yogi**, on his visit to Wardha in August 1935. He writes, "No other leader in the world has attained the secure niche in the hearts of his people that Gandhiji occupies for India's unlettered millions". Swami Yogananda's description of Gandhiji goes as, "The tiny 100 pound saint is radiant in physical, mental and spiritual health. His soft brown eyes sparkle with intelligence, sincerity and discrimination. He mentions Gandhiji's detachment of mind by recalling his appendectomy operation, He chatted cheerfully, with his infectious smile revealing unawareness of pain."

During his two day visit to Wardha, the Yogi asked a few questions to Mahatmaji. On his question, "Mahatma ji you are an exceptional man. How can you expect the world to act as you do". To this Gandhiji replied (p. 433), "I am as frail a mortal as any of us and that I never had anything extraordinary about me nor have I now. I am a simple individual liable to err like any other fellow mortal. I have enough humility to confess my error and to retrace my steps. I own that I have immovable faith in God and His goodness."

On another question Gandhiji said, "I would wait for ages rather than seek the freedom of my country through bloody means". Still on another question Gandhiji said, "I can call myself nationalist but my nationalism is as broad as the universe. It includes in its sweep all the nations on the earth. My nationalism includes the well being of the whole world." In the above statement one can see how Gandhiji's ideas reflect the vedic wisdom. Indian scriptures have said, "My home is this earth".

Tagore respected Gandhiji, yet was critical of many a proposal of Gandhiji. At one place the poet said, "The science and art of building up swaraj is a vast subject. But he came to one narrow field". Mahatma Gandhi's reply to his Gurudeo (respected teacher) is again full of respect, devotion, courtesy and logic. This reply appeared in Young India of 13 October 1921. Gandhi begins his reply:

> *"The Bard of Shantiniketan has contributed to the Modern Review a brilliant essay on the present movement. It is a series of word pictures which he alone can paint. It is an eloquent protest against authority, slave mentality or whatever description one gives of blind acceptance of a passing mania whether out of fear or hope. It is a welcome and wholesome reminder to all workers that we must not be impatient. We must not impose authority no matter how great. The poet tells us summarily to reject anything and everything that does not appeal to our reason or heart."*

With these and much praise for Tagore, the Mahatma boldly but most respectfully asserts that if the country has come to believe in the spinning wheel as the giver of plenty, it has done so after a laborious thinking, after great hesitation. "He must not mistake the surface dirt for the substance beneath.... It is a plea for recognizing the dignity of labour. It was our love of foreign cloth that ousted the wheel from its position of dignity. Therefore, I consider it a sin to wear foreign cloth".

The argument Gandhiji further builds in his reply is that the hungry millions in India ask for invigorating food. They must earn it. And they can earn only by the sweat of their brow. Spinning wheel is the answer. These ideas along with the use of mother tongue in schools, the benefit of doing productive work, the impact of leading frugal and simple life, the need for character formation led to his conceptualization of Nai Taleem in 1937.

The Poona Pact and Dr. Ambedkar: Relationship between Gandhiji and Dr. Ambedkar were warm, friendly and respectful. Gandhiji took fast unto death in September 1932 to avoid balkanizing of India politically. When Dr. Ambedkar met Gandhiji (September 20-24, 1932), he was visibly moved. Gandhiji told him, "You are untouchable by birth, I am untouchable by adoption (Sahare 1988, p. 52). After the Poona Pact, it is reported that Rajaji and Dr. Ambedkar exchanged their pens.

Dr. Ambedkar had participated in all the three Round Table Conferences in London in November 1930, September 1931 and November 1932. Gandhiji made this statement, "From the reports that have reached of your work at RTC, I know you are a patriot of sterling worth". Mutual respect between them was one reason behind signing the Poona Pact.

Babasahib Dr. Bhimrao Ambedkar, was one of the most illustrious sons of India. He is well-known for his massive contribution in framing of the Indian Constitution. His phenomenal work for the betterment of the oppressed classes is also well-known. But his contributions to education and his achievement as a student are known dimly. We highlight that aspect.

Bhimrao Ambedkar was the son of Ramji Sakpal, who was a Subedar in British Army. Bhim was born on 14 April 1891 at Mhow Cantonment. After two years, his father retired from military service and he moved to Satara where his wife died when Bhim was hardly six years of age. Due to sincerity and hard-work as a young student, Bhim won the heart of his teachers. One of the teachers whose surname was Ambedkar always treated him with love. This teacher made him adopt the surname Ambedkar. He passed High School Exam in 1907 with highest marks in Persian. Bhim got married at the age of 16 with a girl whose name was changed to Ramabai (She was much younger in age). After his intermediate examination, the Maharaja of Baroda, granted a scholarship of ₹ 25 which helped him to complete his B.A. in 1913.

The Maharaja of Baroda, looking at his tenacity, intelligence and love for learning, further granted him scholarship to study at Columbia University in U.S.A. where he was awarded M.A. in

1915 for his thesis, "Ancient Indian Commerce". In 1916, he submitted his Ph.D., "The National Dividend of India".

He left New York in 1916 and came to London and entered, in October 1916 Gray's Inn for doing his Bar-at-Law. Also simultaneously he enrolled himself in London School of Economics. But he was asked to come back to Baroda. He reached there in September 1917. In November 1917 he came to Bombay.

With financial help from the Maharaja of Kolhapur and other friends, he could again leave for London in July 1920 to pursue his studies at London School of Economics and was called to bar simultaneously. He completed his thesis "Provincial Decentralization of Finance in British India", for which he was awarded Master of Science in 1921. By October 1922 he completed another thesis on The Problem of Rupee for the University of London, which he was asked to revise. He came to Bombay in April 1923, revised his thesis and sent it. The University of London awarded him Doctor of Science degree in 1923. In 1923, he started his practice as a barrister in Bombay.

Dr. Ambedkar's nationalism and awareness of socio-political events were the consideration for nominating him to the Bombay Legislative Council as a member in January 1927. He also started fortnightly Marathi paper *Bahishkrit Bharat* (बहिष्कृत भारत). Dr. Ambedkar was given the highest distinction to be a member of the Viceroy's Executive Council in July 1942 and was offered Labour Portfolio in the expanded Executive Council. This Council got dissolved in 1946 when the Labour Government came to power in England. In 1946, he started Siddhart College in Bombay and then Milind College in Aurangabad in 1951.

3.7 Multitasking

Gandhiji was greatly impressed by one person; Raichandra or Raj Chandra, who was a jewel merchant but was also a deeply religious person with spiritual orientation. Gandhiji calls him *Satdhyani* (Autob. p. 82), doing hundred things at a time which may also be called as *multitasking*.

Multitasking, in the corporate world, has a narrow meaning. It means an employee besides doing his assigned task also undertakes to perform other tasks and thus additionally helps the firm or the industry. We may give a twist in meaning and define a multitasking person as an individual who listens to the telephonic message, gives dictation to the steno, undertakes brief dialogue with the visitor and also searches out a relevant paper from the pile of files kept on his desk.

Rabindranath Tagore and Gandhiji, both can be put in this category of multitasking individuals. Tagore wrote poems and stories, managed the working of Shantiniketan, directed plays and also undertook acting in the play. Gandhiji often used to dictate letters while spinning along with constant nama japa, *"Ram, Ram"*. When Tagore visited Sabarmati Ashram, Gandhiji was constantly spinning and talking with Tagore on most thoughtful and important issues. Some behavioural psychologists hold that multitasking increases concentration and creativity.

We get a glimpse of Gandhiji's multitasking in the issue of *Young India* dated 23 January 1930, written by Mahadev Desai. Rabindranath Tagore visited Sabarmati Ashram on his mission to collect funds for Vishwa Bharati. Tagore was seventy years of age. He called himself an old man and apologized for taking up much of Gandhiji's time. To this Gandhiji with a smile, replied (Bhattacharya p. 190-191). "An old man of 60 cannot dance but a poet of 70 can dance." When Tagore apologized for taking Gandhiji's time, he replied, "No, you have not wasted my time. I have been spinning without allowing a break in the conversation."

Plate 3.1

During his lifetime and after his death, Gandhiji was a soft target for criticism. He meant different things to different people. Most of the western thinkers saw and evaluated his role as father, husband, friend, social activist, politician and economist. Some people like Winston Churchill criticized him harshly. General Smuts treated him harshly but respected him. Some peeped into his personal life with their coloured glasses. Very few have seen him as a teacher, spiritual person, dedicated to *tyaga, tapa, bhakti* and work. An open-minded person dedicated to *satya, ahimsa* and *aparigraha*. Let us look to what he felt:

- He, who has all but God on his side, has nothing.
- Merit is in fighting alone, be the opponent one or many.
- A devotee is ever absorbed in God.
- We have no existence whatsoever outside and apart from God.
- *Ramnama* is the only unfailing remedy for man's three-fold ills.
- "I do not want my house to be walled in all sides and my windows to be stuffed. I want the cultures of all lands to be blown about my house as freely as possible. But I refuse to be blown off my feet by any".

□

4

Education: An Extended View

- *"Education must be rooted to culture and committed to progress."*

  (UNESCO, 1996)
- *"Teachers affect eternity."*

  (Henry Adams)
- *"To me, the essence of education is concentration of mind."*

  (Swami Vivekananda)
- *"No passion so effectively robs the mind of its powers of reasoning and acting as fear."*

  (Edmund Burke)
- *"The act of progress is to preserve order amidst change and to preserve change amidst order."*

  (A.N. Whitehead)

4.1 Starter

For Gandhij, "education", was much more than reading, writing and arithmetic. The foundation of education was, "character" *charitra*; to do duty, to discharge one's responsibilities, to broaden one's outlook on life, world and work. After solving the political problem of Champaran indigo (*neil*) workers, he concentrated on education and health in six villages. He started schools to promote education among the masses. When the problem of indigo workers of Champaran was satisfactorily solved, he advised his associates that as there was lack of educational facilities in this area they should promote education and set up schools. He discussed this issue with his colleagues. The question was where from to get the teachers, especially teachers of good character. He used his own resources. He called those whom he knew. They included Gandhiji's wife, his son, wife of Mahadeo Desai and a few others. Gandhiji asked them to teach especially healthy habits and moral and ethical behaviour along with literacy. Three teachers were asked to teach health rules to villagers and importance of keeping environment clean. His definition of education was wider than teaching of numeracy and literacy.

Gandhiji's educational activities were not restricted to teachers and schools, he oriented political writers to educate people on health and good behaviour. While promoting सत्याग्रह in 1918, Mahatma Gandhi circulated a set of instructions to *Satyagrahies*. He strongly emphasized that a *satyagrahi* will utter no harsh word, abide by the truth and will not treat with scorn people who hold different views. In a letter of April 1918 (Iyer p. 314-5), he says, "A *satyagrahi* must create opportunities to teach the village children. They must educate villagers about rules of good health and general hygiene and also try to help in solving domestic quarrels among the villagers".

Along with literacy, Gandhiji always recommended teaching of value education. In his speech at YMCA, Madras (*The Hindu* February 16, 1916), he elaborated Ashram vows and brought out the point that one must not possess more than what one needs. If we do that, we are thieves. When millions of Indian do not get one square meal a day, we have no right to enjoy a sumptuous dinner of five courses. We must adjust our necessities. We have basic needs that are to be fulfilled; but we must reduce our necessities and renounce our desires. This idea can be graphically presented. Simplification of life, for Gandhiji, was the highest type of education.

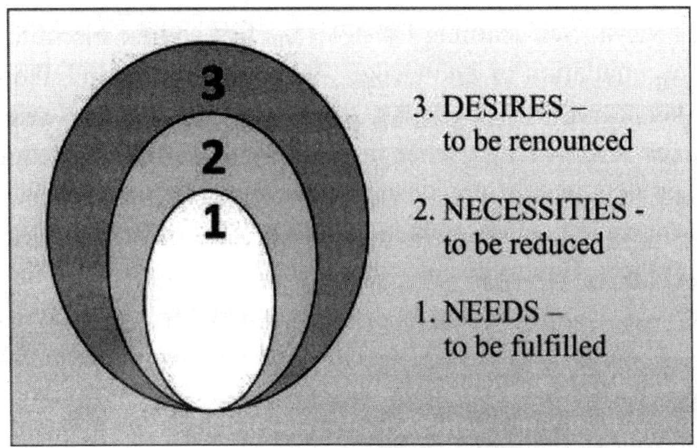

4.2 Social Cohesion and Harmony

The value of peace and social cohesion was the uppermost value with Gandhiji. In a letter addressed to Hakim Ajmal Khan, (Andrews 2006 p. 284-6), he emphasized the point that without Hindu-Muslim unity we cannot attain freedom. The unity demands deep faith in non-violence. In the letter he widens the canvass of non-violence; "Non-violence implies utter humility and goodwill even towards our bitterest opponent".

Hindu-Muslim unity or Inter-faith respect was also a part of education of children at the Tolstoy Farm. He mentions that during the fast in *Ramzan*, arrangements were made for evening meals after sunset. To keep company with Muslims students others also agreed to take meals in the evening. He writes, "I do not remember that there ever was a quarrel much less a split between Hindu and Muslim students on the score of religion" (Andrews p. 148). One of the foremost functions of education is to respect other religions so as to develop social cohesion, social relationship and social capital. His life and work is a living example.

4.3 Self-learning

For self-growth, for self-actualization, for professional development, life-long self-learning is a sure answer. One should not procrastinate and feel indifferent to self-learning and sharing one's views. Self-learning स्वाध्याय is the first and the essential step for accumulation of knowledge. Taitriya Upanishad (1.11) says स्वाध्याय प्रवचनाभ्यां न प्रमदितव्यम्. When one has consulted relevant sources of knowledge, when one has discussed matters with wise and prudent people, one develops one's own points of view. This may be called self-knowledge आत्मज्ञान. This ought to be shared with others. Gandhiji said, "Learn as if you have to live for 100 years and serve as if you have to die tomorrow". The word प्रमाद has two connotation; one, feeling lazy, two, undertaking useless, purposeless unmeaningful activities. The thrust of the above *upnisadnic* quote is to learn and share. Accumulate knowledge and share it with others.

> *"Anyone who stops learning is old, whether at 20 or 80. Anyone who keeps learning stays young. The greatest thing in life is to keep your mind young."*
>
> *(Henry Ford)*

We learn through four activities–observation, reading, listening and self-reflection. We learn a lot if we are mindful observers. We learn when we read, we learn when we listen to wise people. The Kath Upanishad (1.3.14) says: उतिष्ठत जाग्रत प्राप्य वरान्निबोधत । Get up, awake up, be attentive, go to the wise and the learned people and seek the true knowledge. A good student has innate curiosity and a burning desire to learn. A good teacher must read widely, observe carefully and transform his life. We may recall the meaning of *acharya*. Indian scriptures say that an *acharya* (आचार्य) is he one who consults various scriptures and builds his point of view. On that point of view he himself conducts his actions. Such a person is an *acharya*.

No education is self-contained, unless we supplement it by self-learning. It includes mindfulness, observation, thoughtful discussion and deep reflection.

4.4 Man and Nature

Education is meaningless unless it helps people to built respect and reverence for nature. Indian tradition respects environment and sees it as a part of life. Our contemporary education system has been quite alert and alive to the problems. School curriculum (NCERT 1988 p. 25), has advocated, "Genuine concern sensitivity and ability necessary for the preservation and protection of physical and natural resources". NCERT (2000 p. 36) further emphasized that environment sensitivity be developed by integrating the theme (preservation, protection and development of environment), with all teaching subjects. Fundamental Duties 51A lists protection and preservation of environment as one of the duties for all citizens. The Supreme Court of India in their judgement on 18 December 2003 desired that environmental education must be an integral part of education and authority must see that all institutions comply with this order. A part of the judgement is reproduced in the box below:

> *".....the authorities so concerned shall duly supervise such implementation in every educational institution and the non-compliance of the same by any of the institutions shall be treated as an disobedience, calling for instituting disciplinary action against such institution."*
>
> *(The Supreme Court of India Judgement December 18, 2003 in Writ Petition No. 860 of 1991)*

There are two divergent concepts in relation to man's relation to Nature.

Anthropocentric view maintains that the nature is to help the individual and the society, thus man has the right to use nature for his growth, development and earnings. Another view, **Anthropocosmic** considers that man and nature are interdependent and thus man must not exploit nature, should not destroy it, but work to protect it and preserve it. Gandhiji stood for anthropocosmic view. He always stood for protecting environment. If individuals believe in non-accumulation (*aparigraha*), if individuals reduce their desires and necessities, they help protection and preservation of environment.

Gandhiji's concept goes even beyond these two perceptions. His faith is based on the Gita's concept that **prakriti** and **purush** are interconnected, both of them are eternal and comes from *Purushottam* (Gita 13.19).

When there was earthquake in Bihar, Gandhiji said it is the consequence of our ill deeds. The statement was greatly criticized by many including R.N. Tagore and Pandit Jawaharlal Nehru. Nonetheless Gandhiji struck to his proposition and said, "I make no distinction between living and natural forces. We all are guided by the Will of God".

A concept is now in vogue called as **Deep Ecology**. Capra (1996) and Pojman (1998) observed that we may know the harm of exploiting nature but our attitude do not change. Knowing full well that natural resources are limited, we need not destroy ecological balance, we must preserve and protect environment, but when it comes to action, we hardly do anything. Our attitude can change if we realize deeply that nature and living being are an integral whole. Focus on organic interdependency of cosmic forces may change our attitude for eco balance.

Awareness of macro issues relating to eco balance need appropriate knowledge and attitudinal change. If we ponder on some of the following points, we may realize the consequence of our mindless actions:

- Resources are limited.
- They are rapidly declining.
- Unless we change our consumption habits, we will not be able to keep up the eco balance.

Gandhiji believed in all these above statements. He succinctly said, **"Nature has enough for our need not for our greed"**. With reference to deep ecology, we may, here, refer to a historical fact that faithfully echoed, long back, the true Gandhian perspective. In 1854, the President of the United States, made an offer of money for a large area of land and promised a, "reservation", of a chunk for the Indian people. The Red Indian Leader, Seattle Chief, gave a long reply. Tagore paid the highest tribute to the letter saying, "It is a piece of poem in which several Tagores and Wordsworths have been rolled up in one". We give below a few selective sentences and excerpts:

"Promise that you and your children will not disturb the peace of forests. Promise that you and your children will not pollute the scented air and the waters. Promise that you will not press out the beautiful wrinkles from the face of our mother Earth. Promise that you will not humble the brethren animals to extinction. This is the only price we would like to charge for the land."

4.5 Language Matters

Gandhiji was an expert of expression; clear, concise and forceful. The term passive resistence was changed to *satyagraha* in South Africa. In India during 1919-21, he used the expression non-cooperation which he says (Autob. p. 444), "Became a current coin". Later on he coined another term "Civil disobedience", which was in vogue till 1942. Then came the sure and forceful term **Quit India**. These terms are brief and pointed yet forceful and action centric.

The other expression he raised was in 1930. On March 12, 1930, he along with 78 volunteers set out to *Dandi* on the sea coast, 241 miles from Sabarmati. His expression for this occasion was:

"I want world sympathy in this battle of Right against Might."

Dandi (M.K. Gandhi)
dated 5.4.1930

On returning from London Round Table Conference (RTC), in 1931, he said, "I have returned empty-handed but did not allow the prestige of India to be damaged". When Winston Churchill called him half-naked *fakir*, his reaction was most positive.

Gandhiji was an educationist par excellence. We now look at the language aspect of Gandhiji to show that he was not only a deep thinker but also a clear communicator. The first example relates to formulation of the Constitution of Indian National Congress which, as he says, was his real entrance into the organization.

Before 1919, the constitution of Congress was the gift of Prof. Gokhale. He had prepared some rules and regulations for the Congress party which were being followed. However, all leaders were of the view that a new constitution needs to be prepared. He say (Autob. p. 448), "The Congress leaders had found that *I had a faculty for condensed expression*". The task was given to Gandhiji and he did it well. As a writer and organizer, he was well-known among leaders like Lokmanya B.G. Tilak, Madan Mohan Malaviya, Motilal Nehru and Desh Bandhu. Although there were three members on the new drafting committee, most of the work was done by Gandhiji alone; although he did consult the other two, Lokmanya and Desh Bandhu. With the assumption of this responsibility he made real entrance into the Congress politics.

The second instance relates to indentured labour. Indentured labour was sent to other countries after signing bond with the British authorities. This system was prevailing in India and Pandit Madan Mohan Malaviya, in 1916, raised this issue in the General Assembly. Lord Hardinge, the Viceroy assured that this Act will be abolished in due course. Gandhiji was not satisfied with this expression. He, therefore, had a meeting in Bombay to impress upon the government to tell specially when this law will be repelled. There were three proposals; as soon as possible, by the 31st July, immediate abolition. Gandhiji's proposal was for 31 July. The government agreed on repelling the law before July 31. They did on 31 May 1917.

The third instance relates about the term, "Passive Resistance". Gandhiji used this term in South Africa. The Hindi translation is *nishkriya pratirodha* निष्क्रिय प्रतिरोध, which was not describing the approach accurately. The term was born in South Africa in 1908. A Gujarati speaking friend suggested the term and it was adjudged the best (Iyer p. 308).

One of the major concerns of any Indian top educationist is to think deeply and clearly on national language. Different languages are spoken in different parts of the country. English had the strong backing of the government. On 21 January 1918, Gandhiji wrote a letter to "Gurudev", Tagore and sought his opinion on these points:

- Is not Hindi (Hindustani) the only possible national language for interprovincial intercourse and for all national proceedings?

- Should not Hindi be the language principally used at the forthcoming Congress?
- Is it not desirable and possible to give the highest teaching in our schools through vernacular?

This letter speaks of the concern of an educationist for a common national language; though Swami Daya Nanda Saraswati and Iswar Chand Vidya Sagar earlier had strongly advocated for the use of vernacular. And with success.

4.6 Prayer Meetings: A Reflective Teaching Strategy

Gandhiji used to educate himself and others through prayer meetings held both in the morning as well as in the evening. He would do so in Ashram, in prison as well as while travelling. In the morning he would himself meditate as well listen to *bhajans* and *slokas* and poems from other religions. In the evening prayer meetings, he will address the gathering on a social, political point. Religious aspect of these meetings included:

- The first *sloka* of Ishovasya Upanishad.
- Newman's prayer: "One step enough for me".
- Islamic prayer.
- Jain and Buddhist prayers.
- The last 18 *slokas* of II chapter of the Gita.
- A *bhajan* by the poet Narsi Mehta, वैष्नव जन तो तेने कहिये जो पीर पराई जाणे रे was the choicest *bhajan* of Gandhiji.

4.7 Humility: Foundation of Education

Indian scriptures have outlined values. Keeping those in view Gandhiji prepared a list and circulated to the members of Sabarmati Ashram. One of the members (Gurudas Banerji), suggested that humility should be given a place in the list of vows. However, it was not included. Gandhiji had his own views on humility because it cannot be practiced. He argued that truth, non-violence, fearlessness, local products (सत्य, अहिंसा, अभय, सवदेशी), are to be practiced. To feel that one is humble makes one hypocrite. A humble person himself is not conscious of his humbleness.

Humility is to make oneself zero. Humility cannot be learned by formal training. Etiquette and good behaviour is not humility. Let us look at three great examples of humility. We start with Mahatma Gandhi.

Gandhiji was a great devotee of truth and non-violence. He had the rare courage to live the truth he learnt. *Satyagraha* and *Sarvodaya* were the two most significant contributions in the area of political and social life of India of 1915 to 1948. He lived by the idea of *Satya* and *Ahimsa*. Fearlessness and malicelessness were his *pranic* force. In 1924, he requested Mohammed Yakub to desist from moving Assembly resolution recommending award of Nobel Peace Prize to him. When people coined the word Gandhian, he, in his disarming simplicity, said, Forget Gandhi and Gandian. "I have said nothing new. Truth and non-violence are as old as hills".

The second illustration is from *Prasna Upanishad*. Six renowned Rishis go to Piplada and ask him questions about Bhraham. He answers all questions; and at the end he says, "I know only this much". एतावदेवाहम् तत्परं ब्रह्मवेद (प्र. 3 6). It is an expression of the height of humility.

The third, well-known example of humility, is an expression by Isaac Newton. He was considered the topmost scientist of the world in his lifetime. When people showered praise on him, he in his characteristic modesty said, "He was but a child playing at the seashore while the immense ocean of truth lay all unexplored before him". On another occasion he said, "If I have seen farther it is by standing on shoulders of the giants" and "If I have done the public any service it is due to patient thought".

A sense of humility is the gateway of knowledge and good behaviour. The more we learn, the more we realize the extent and depth of our ignorance. Our knowledge of ignorance propels us to seek more knowledge. This is the essence of the expression, vidya leads to humility, modesty विद्या ददाति विनयम्। With humility we extend and enlarge our capability to learn विनयम् ददाति पात्रताम्।

Bottery and Wright (2000) advises us to be guided by intellectual humility (ज्ञानात्मक विनम्रता) and reflective integrity

(वैचारिक अखंडता). As human beings we do not have infinite powers to think and reason. There might be occasions when we may misjudge and miscalculate. Further in our thinking we borrow and use thinking of others also. These aspects lead us to intellectual humility.

Reflective integrity involves limitation of our perception. Our perceptions are shaped by our education, training and experiences. Further, as our experiences and exposure grow and change, they bring changes in our perceptions also. Thus perceptions evolve. This aspect must make us open to other perceptions.

4.8 Seven Social Evils

It may not be an exaggeration to say the literates of India are gradually putting the great legacy of Gandhian thought and ideas on the back burner. They are getting drifted away from his teachings. If we look at the world of commerce, or education or politics, we will see that commerce hardly keeps morality in view; that education rarely attempts to develop character of the learner and in politics people play the game without following basic principles of *live and let live*. Country is more than party, development is more than economic growth, understanding is more than assertiveness. As we all want to build a strong India, we need to remedy the situation quickly and fully. Gandhiji showed us the way.

With his unalloyed faith in truth and non-violence Gandhiji's vision was holistic, multidimensional and focused on the good of the poorest of the poor. With his penetrating intellect, ever evolving and ever widening, Gandhiji saw gaping holes in various areas of life and spoke candidly about them. He was the person whom Nehru describes as *"Powerful current of fresh air that made us stretch ourselves and take deep breaths, like a beam of light that pierced the darkness and removed the scales from our eyes, like whirlwind that upsets many things but most of all the working of people's mind"* (Shanker 1993 p. 63).

In the seven social evils, Gandhiji delineated that commerce and trade focus more attention on profit and production, and rarely on moral issues connected with trade and commerce including improvement of working conditions of the labour force. In education, the planners, administrations and teachers focus on cognitive development of the learner and not on building his character, and *samskars*. In politics, people take segmental view which does not result into the good of all. Politics does not follow principle of *sarve bhuta hite rata* सर्व भूत हिते रता। (The Gita 5.24, 12.4).

1. Commerce without morality
2. Education without character
3. Pleasure without conscience
4. Politics without principle
5. Science without humanity
6. Wealth without work
7. Worship without service.

Gandhiji by nature was not a dry personality. He would not shun joys and pleasures of life and living. But he would say, "Do it in moderation and with mindfulness. The Gita (6.17) advices us *Yukta aahara viharashyaca.* Follow the dictate of the inner conscience. He was of the view that science with its mind boggling discoveries and inventions must never lose sight of humanity. Gandhiji never appreciated earning wealth that does not involve work and worship that does not include service. His list of seven social evils is given in the box."

The above brief, clear and succinct expressions are *sutras* of great value. Gandhiji had a gift of brevity that contained deep-seated richness of emotions and intellect. About his language and expression, he said, "My language is aphoristic, it lacks precision". It is open, therefore, to many interpretation. His reply and comment on UNESCO's Draft Resolution on Human Rights sent to him by Aldoux Huxley contains more than what was expressed. He wrote, "His wise but illiterate mother has taught him that if everyone does his **duty**, everyone else will get his **rights**".

Many Nobel Laureates are of the view that problems of 21st century in the field of economics and environmental sciences can be solved by following Gandhian principles. On his farsightedness, simplicity and catholicity of outlook remarks of Albert Einstein are worth recalling, *"The future generations may find it hard to believe that such a person ever walked on earth in flesh and blood".*

Gandhiji's identification of seven sins is an example of his futuristic vision of life and living. Let us now elaborate a bit on, Seven Social Evils. I express my gratitude to Prof. J.S. Rajput, who helped me massively.

• **Commerce Without Morality:** Industrial houses and the corporate world keep their eyes on profit and production. Their ethical and moral responsibility towards their workforce hardly gets due attention, with the result that wages of the workers are low and working condition shocking and appalling. In this maxim Gandhiji advises the industrial houses to keep in view social concern and concerns of the workforce. Here, we may recall that Gandhiji undertook an agitation against mill-owners in Ahmedabad as they were paying low wages to the labour. Gandhiji stood with workers although all the mill-owners had deep respect for Gandhiji and many of them were most close to him. Unmindful of personal relations Gandhiji threw himself on the side of workers. In the end mill-owners gave in and agreed to provide increase in the wages of the workers. Some of the thoughtful industrial houses now do keep morality in view besides profits and product. When Dr. Abdul Kalam asked Azim Premji what is the secret of his quick success, he replied, "Along with economic profit we kept in view social concerns" (Abdul Kalam, 2003). This is what all industrial houses need to do, as Indian tradition talks about *subha labha.*

• **Education Without Character:** Modern education in India which started with Macaulay in 1835 was memory-oriented and information centric. In Gandhiji's view, cognitive learning that strengthens mental faculty is only a small part of education. True education ought to develop hand, head and heart (what he also called as body, mind and spirit). In Gandhiji's view book teaching is one small role of schools. Their major role is to develop character of students that include development of right values, positive attitudes, healthy mindset and right *samskars*. A.N. Whitehead said, education must inculcate sense of doing one's duty and respect to others (Whitehead, 1970 p. 23). Swami Vivekanand said, "The aim of education is concentration of mind". Dr. Albert Einstein's views come close to Gandhiji's view. He said, "We should not make intellect our God. It cannot lead. It can only serve".

Gandhiji in his role as father ensured that the education he provided to his children made them good human beings. His view on the aspect is very clear in his Autobiography (in the chapter "Tares among wheat"). In a certain discussion, Dr. D.S. Kothari who was the Chairman, National Education Commission 1964-66 and entitled the Report as Education for National Development said, "If he had another chance to chair National Commission on Education," he would entitle it as, "Education for Character Development".

- **Pleasure Without Conscience:** Gandhiji was a person who would not shun joy, pleasure and happiness of life. For him life itself was a joyful and a pleasurable experience but it needs to be guided and controlled by dictate of the conscience; what he called as "inner voice". As a believer of the Gita he loved युक्त आहार-विहार (6.17). He also believed in the Gita that one can enjoy pleasures of life provided they are in tune with and not opposed to "dharma". धर्मविरुद्धो भुतेषु कमोऽस्मि भरतर्षम (7.11)

Gandhiji was a person who appreciated self-discipline and put restrictions on his life. He imposed self-discipline for leading good and purposeful life. Galbraith (1983, p. 20) has remarked that in Harvard University the outgoing graduates speak a statement in Convocation. *"There are wise restrictions that make men happy"*. Gandhiji was one who would always do that. His eleven vows were:

अहिंसा सत्य अस्तेय ब्रह्मचर्य असंग्रह
शरीर श्रम अस्वाद सर्वत्र भयवर्जन
सर्वधर्म समानत्य स्वदेशी स्पर्श भावना
विनम्र व्रत निष्ठा सेयेएकादश सेव्य हैं।

For Gandhiji pleasures ought to be regulated and controlled by conscience. Let me close this point with a real incident. Some Americans visited **Sewagram**. They talked, lived and closely watched his daily schedule of work that started at 3.45 a.m. At the end of their visit, these visitors said, "You lead a very hectic life.

Why don't you go for a holiday." Gandhiji's reply was, "I am always on a holiday". He loved work. And work provided him joy and meaning of life. For him work was a prayer to God, for him work was an offering to God. The Gita says one who dedicates his work to God and does his activities without attachment (and not craving for results), to such a person sins do not touch as water does not touch the lotus leaf.

• **Politics Without Principles:** The vision of Gandhiji was farsighted, broad and holistic. He was truly a religious person who loved to serve one and all without distinction. He took to politics not to gain some personal or party benefits but to fight injustice and maintain autonomy and dignity of the individual. His work in South Africa was against apartheid as he strongly believed that, "All men are created equal". He was against all kinds of dominance. His work in India was based on the principle that no race should enslave another race and other people. If there is a foreign power in a country then the role of the foreign power must be for the benefits of the governed and not against them. He felt that it is the duty of every citizen to oppose the evil and cooperate with the good. Non-cooperation with the evil is as much a duty as cooperation with the good.

If the politicians work for the good of one party, they exclude the good of people of other parties. This is a dangerous and narrow way of looking at national issues. Politics must always be guided by principles. It must take care of the poorest of the poor and the marginalized lot. Gains through politics for the self or for the party are trivial. Good of all must be the goal. Well being of all must be the motto.

• **Science Without Humanity:** Science is the continuation of eternal human urge to search, explore, understand and utilize. It has reached a stage when it can make life easier and free from drudgery. Further, it has provided tools to explore further, and understand nature better. Science must remain humane. It should help remove hunger and poverty. It should create no more Hiroshimas and Nagasakis. Gandhian thoughts on this aspect provide us in-depth understanding on the role of science. Science must serve humanity. Science need not ignore ethical issues. Science has helped us to gain knowledge about outer space but has not helped us in exploring the inner space.

• **Wealth Without Work:** Gandhiji read John Ruskin's book, "Unto the Last", while on train from Johannesburg to Durban. He was so impressed by the contents of the book that when he got down at Durban he decided to live those principles in his life (Autobiography p. 275). He mentally resolved to reduce principles to practice.

For Gandhiji wealth earned without putting personal effort and labour is no wealth at all. Wealth earned with work and labour has its own taste and sweatiness. Eating without physical labour is stealing.

• **Worship Without Service:** Fully dedicated to truth and non-violence Gandhiji always looked at the core of the central issue and not at marginal and peripheral points. Worship, meditation, bhakti are good. They help individual in his journey to spiritualism. But these individual activities must be supported by service rendered to the society what Sri Krishna, in the Gita, calls as *Loka Sangraha* लोक संग्रह (3.20). Gandhiji attached great significance to service. In his Autobiography he mentioned two instances when he worked as bearer (buttoning up the coat of the congress secretary and working as clerk sorting out letters in Calcutta Congress Session of 1901). Throughout his life Gandhiji worked for the good of the untouchables. At some place he says, "In matters of learning, learn as if you have to live for 100 years and in matters of service serve as if you have to die the next day". One incident is well-known. Pt. Nehru and other national leaders were discussing with Gandhiji very serious national issues. They were surprised when they saw Gandhiji leaving the meeting. "Where are you going Bapu?". "To dress the leg of the goat", he said.

4.9 Hind Swaraj and Education

Hind Swaraj, a small booklet, was written by Mahatma Gandhi in 1908 on his return to South Africa from England. The original was in Gujarati and was first published in the columns of *Indian Opinion* in 1909. It is a book that expresses Gandhiji's own thoughts rejecting School of Violence. In his considered opinion violence is no remedy for India's ills. What he wrote was appreciated. Miss Irene Rathbone observes: "Hind Swaraj is an enormously powerful book" and further says that, "By virtue of its tremendous honesty, she was forced to search her own honesty". She advises, "I will implore people to read it" (Hind Swaraj p. 12). When Gokhale saw this book in 1912 in South Africa he prophesied that Gandhiji himself will destroy the book after spending a year in India. But his prophesy and prediction failed. Gandhiji only altered one word at the request of a British Lady. This book advocates the gospel of love in place of hate. It replaces violence by self-sacrifice. It pits soul force against brute force.

Many people made sharp comments on Gandhiji's views on Western Civilization and the use of machinery. Middleton Murry observed that Gandhiji's spinning wheel is a machine, and so also spectacles on the nose. The plough is machine. Later on Gandhiji clarified that he is against machinery because it makes thousands of people go without work. This machinery concentrates wealth in the hands of a few; it snatches dignity, worth and working capacity of the poor. In, A Message of July 14, 1938, he says even after 30 years he holds the same line of thought. In a light vein he also says that the reader ought to balance my views with the opinion of a dear friend that, "It was the production of a fool" (Hind Swaraj, p. 17).

Before coming to the major contents of Hind Swaraj, we would like to go to the root of the word Swaraj. One who knows oneself, knows Brahman and realizes Him. Such a person possess self-rule आप्नोति स्वराज्यम्। Such a person becomes one's own master and does not get guided by forces of outer nature (प्रकृति) but get regulated by his own will, the soul force. R.W. Emerson said, "Education of the will is the object of our existence". With self-efforts and perseverance such a person "Manifests the perfection already in man". The Gita (14.24) uses another term *swastha*

(स्वस्थ); one who considers gain and loss, victory and defeat; joy and pain, praise and blame, friend and foe with a tranquil, calm and peaceful mind. The mind that is equipoised is considered as settled in itself *swastha*.

Hind Swaraj (note the spelling it is swaraj), (स्वराज) not swarajya (स्वराज्य) has twenty chapters; short, brief and pointedly written. Right in the beginning Gandhiji makes a succinct declaration on the objectives of a newspaper; which, essentially he followed throughout his life.

- Understand popular feelings and give expression to it.
- Arouse among the people desirable sentiments.
- Fearlessly expose popular defects.

If we look at these three objectives of journalism, we see Gandhiji as life-couch or life skills couch, or behaviour modifier or personal growth consultant. While explaining the good work of Congress in achieving Home Rule, he appreciates the role of O. Hume William Wedderburn, Dadabhai Noroji and Gokhale. The partition of Bengal by Lord Curzon in 1905 started the national unrest or discontent. Gandhiji ridicules parliament and quoting Carlyle calls it a, "Talking shop of the world" and a costly toy. He ridicules Western Civilization and calls it as a seven day wonder.

In the chapter. "Why was India lost", he takes the stand that the English has not taken India. We have given India to them. His views also on the role of railways, doctors, lawyers are unique and original.

On education he has stated that we have limited its role by saying that it is means to knowledge of letters (p. 77). The existing system of education does not make men of us. It does not enable us to do our duty. Mahatma Gandhi did not run down knowledge of letters. But he did not consider it *Kamadhenu*. Character building ought to have the first place in education. He liked the definition of education as given in the box.

Gandhiji believed in man-making education that inculcates the urge and willingness to do duty truthfully and without self-interest.

> *"That man I think has had a liberal education who has been so trained in youth that his body is the ready-servant of his will ..., whose intellect is clear ..., whose mind is stored with a knowledge of the fundamental truths of nature ..., whose passions are trained to come to heel by a vigorous will..., who has learned to hate all vileness and to respect others as himself........"*
>
> *(Hind Swaraj p. 78)*

"Education is the right of all; man and woman, young and old, poor and rich. Education is our right as well as our duty. It is our *swadharma* (स्वधर्म). We ought to educate ourselves throughout our lives using every experience, every observation. We ought to use all our senses to educate us. We ought to use both our mind and heart, our reason and intuition. Education has eternal as well as instrumental values. It is only through education that we develop the society economically, socially, culturally and spiritually. Such an education demands *viveka* to discriminate between truth and untruth, good and bad; grain and chaff.

Education has multiple objectives. It must develop and enhance our material prosperity, it must promote our aesthetic sensibility, it must promote intellectual rigour and creativity, it must enkindle deeper love for spirituality. Above all, irrespective of circumstances, it must infuse energy, enthusiasm, perseverance and patience धृति उत्साह समन्वित (Gita 18.26). In short education is an instrument for the transformation of the self, and the society, leading to individual and collective development.

Education also demands a lot from the individual. In one word it demands *tyaga, tapa, tapasya* त्याग, तप, तपस्या. There are no short-cuts in education, no fast food counters in education. If we want quick gains bad is our bargain. Let these things sink in our minds.

At the end of this book *Hind Swaraj*, Gandhiji lists more than a dozen crisp points and emphasizes the point that if we become fearless and say what we exactly think and face the consequences then we shall be able to impress with our speech. No nation has risen without suffering. Let us know that action is better than speech. Let each of us do our duty. He ends with the wise words.

"If I do my duty I shall be able to serve others. Home rule is self rule or self-control."

In *Hind Swaraj*, Gandhiji attacks modern civilization. He considers it a bane that has developed an infinite multiplicity of wants. Modernization is visible in economics, with emphasis on mass production, innovations, entrepreneurship, resulting into mass unemployment and no dignity to labour and the individual. It is visible in politics; with its emphasis on centralization, bureaucracy, party loyalty and mutual disrespect. Socially, modernization is visible in mobility, individualization, urbanization, fast transport. Epistemologically it demand respect to reason and disregard to tradition, intuition and culture. Gandhiji thus was against modern civilization.

4.10 Gandhiji's Educational Fads

Gandhiji in his disarming humility says that the result of his "Educational fads", is in the womb of the future (Autob. p. 185). He even goes to the extent of accepting and owning undesirable traits of his eldest son. He writes (Autob. p. 185), "I have always felt that the undesirable traits, I see today in my eldest son are the echo of my undisciplined and unformulated yearly life. I regard that time as a period of half-baked knowledge and indulgence". He makes another remark (Autob. p. 186) to bring out the major objectives of education, "Had I been without a sense of self-respect and satisfied myself with having given education for my children that other children could not get, I shall have deprived them of the object lessons in liberty and self-respect that I gave them at the cost of the literary training. And when where a choice has to be made between liberty and learning who will not say that the former has to be preferred a thousand times to the latter".

Liberty v/s Learning: In a thoughtful book Ronald J. Terchek brings out the point that, "Autonomy stands at the centre of Gandhi's political philosophy" (Terchek, 2000 p. 21). Aim of education for Gandhiji was to develop and sustain liberty, inner freedom and autonomy. Autonomy has two meanings for Gandhiji. One, individuals must be able to survive physically. They must have food, shelter and clothing. By putting in honest labour they can keep their bodies and soul together. Either the individuals should explore their work or the society must provide them work. Need of spinning and weaving is an answer.

The second meaning is one must be fearless and have courage to speak his mind clearly and boldly. One has not to be a slave of another person. Individuals need to be self-governing and fearless. In *Hind Swaraj* this is the basic point Gandhiji brings out. He is not only interested in decolonization, in kicking the tiger out of India, he wants Indians to be masters of themselves, and their actions. They are at present slaves of their emotions like fear, sycophancy, envy, jealously, untruth. He wanted everyone to be fearless, honest, cooperative, kind, helpful and dedicated to truth.

Learning concentrates on cognitive learning or literary training of school subjects. It was this trend that he advised students to leave schools and colleges as they were getting, "miseducation". It was this which goaded him to announce the scheme of Basic Education or Nai Taleem in 1937.

We have a letter (dated March 28, 1932) from Gandhiji (Iyer p. 71-73) that relates to Ruskin's views on Education. At the end of the letter Gandhiji wishes that a time may come when Gujarati writers may write like Ruskin. He says, "But a time will certainly come when the love of our language will have become Universal and we shall have written like Ruskin and will have as powerful Gujarati as the English of Ruskin" (p. 73). Gandhiji also listed six ideas of Ruskin relating to core aspects of education. Every student must keep **air, water and earth** clean and unpolluted and every student must have **three virtues of gratitude, hope and charity**.

Let us make a short comment on Gandhiji's desire that Gujarati in future must become a powerful language as the English of Ruskin. In 1930s, all Indian languages were seen as second rate languages and English was given the highest regard. Modern education that started in 1835 gave no place to vernacular. Thanks to dedicated efforts of Iswar Chand Vidyasagar and then Swami Dayanand Saraswati that vernacular language was also used along with English in Schools and Colleges. We may also recall

Gandhiji's speech at the opening of Banaras Hindu University in February 1916 when he said, "I am ashamed that I talk in language that is foreign to me."

Gandhiji's keen desire was that India's regional languages must become world-class in content, thought, expression and style. It is a great pity to see that his dream has still not been realized.

4.11 Some Quotes on Education

The term "Education" or *Vidya* has a deeper and wider connotation. It is not only a human right but it is a duty for all. It helps society to promote all items of development. As observed by UNESCO (2001 p. 7), education helps, "In reducing poverty, promoting health, sharing technology, protecting environment, promoting gender equality, extending democracy and improving governance". Education is a process of cultivating positive traits of personality and removing the negative ones. It leads to *abhyudaya* or what Prof. Sen (2005) calls as self well being. It is "A process of being what we are not" (Chattopadhyaya 2001). It is a process of becoming man as observed in Rig Veda (x.53.6) *Manurabhava janaya daivyajanam* मनुर्भव: जनया दैव्या जनम् ।

- "Education of the will is the object of our existence".

  R.W. Emerson
- "Education is the manifestation of the perfection already in man".

  Swami Vivekananda
- "To educate a person in mind and not in morals is to add menace to society".

  Roosevelt
- "Education is a progressive discovery of our ignorance".

  Will Durand
- "The empires of the future are the empires of the mind".

  W. Churchill
- "Education must not only inform but inspire".

  R.N. Tagore
- "With wisdom grows doubt".

  JWV Goethe

- "Education is not for knowing more but behaving differently."

  John Ruskin

- "Science is organized knowledge, wisdom is organized living".

  Immanual Kant

- "The most important aim of education is to make young think".

  Albert Schweitzer

- "Education is a dual task of restitution and renovation".

  UNESCO 1972

- "The illiterates of the 21 century will not be those who cannot read and write but those who cannot unlearn and relearn".

  Alvin Toffler

- "It is a miracle that our curiosity survives formal education".

  Albert Einstein

- "I have never allowed my schooling interfere my education".

  Mark Twain

- "Education is not filling a bucket but lighting a fire".

  W.B. Yeats

- "The capacity to learn is the capacity to alter what one is and has been. It places the present at risk".

  Scheffler

- "Education is the ability to listen to almost anything without losing your temper or your self-confidence".

  Robert Frost

- "Good people improve themselves ceaselessly".

  Confucious

- "There are only two lasting bequests we can give to our children, one is roots, the other wings".

  Stephen Covey

- "The secret of education lies in respecting the student".

  R.W. Emerson

- "Spiritual dimension has to be given the central importance".

  UNESCO 1996
- "Let us become the change we seek in the world".

  M.K. Gandhi
- "Education should be an exposure to greatness".

  A.N. Whitehead
- "A professor is an ignorant man thinking actively utilizing his small store of knowledge".

  A.N. Whitehead
- "Elevate yourself by your own efforts".

  H.D. Thoreau
- "Character building has the first place in education and that is primary education".

  M.K. Gandhi
- "University is a place where adventure of thought must meet the adventure of action."

  A.N. Whitehead
- "Speak the truth to the powerful
Make the truth powerful
Make the powerful truthful."

  Jeremy Cronin
South African Communist Leader

□

5

Leave Schools and Colleges

- *"I have given many things to India. But this system of education together with its techniques, I feel, is the best of them. I do not think I will have anything better to offer to the country."*

  Gandhiji's remark at the Wardha Conference, 1937 (NCTE 1999 p. 86)
- *"Mass illiteracy is India's sin and shame and must be liquidated. Of course, literacy campaign must not begin and end with mere knowledge of letters".*

  (NCTE 1999 p. 177)
- *"The medium of instruction should be altered at once at any cost, the provincial languages be given their rightful place".*

  (NCTE 1999 p. 143)

5.1 Starter

When Gandhiji came back from South Africa to India in 1915, English education imparted in all schools and colleges, was so designed as not to develop values of patriotism, nationalism and Indian identity. Some national initiatives designed to develop national identity and Indian culture were operating but they were only a few islands on the vast ocean of valueless education. Bold initiatives, to name a few, were Shantiniketan, DAV Schools, and institutions run by National Council of Education, Bengal. Sri

Aurobindo educational innovations began in Pondicherry after 1911.

Education in schools and colleges run by Government of India included history and geography of Europe and achievements of the British Empire. Education was basically memory-oriented and anglocentric. Gandhiji noted this distortion and realized that it was more of miseducation than education. He, during 1919, asked students to leave schools and colleges. But before we go to details in this matter, let us briefly look into the history of English Education that began in 1835, along with its ideology and the personal perception of its founding father, T.B. Macaulay.

5.2 Macaulay's Educational Design

After the death of Mughal Emperor, Aurangzeb in 1707, East India Company became powerful and in 1757 Lord Clive (1725-1774) defeated Nawab Sirajuddowlah in the battle of Plassey, and became the Master of Bengal. After twenty years or so the Company assumed sovereignty over Bihar and Orissa by defeating Shah Allam II (in 1764) in the battle of Buxer. *Dewani* rights of Bengal, Bihar and Orissa were granted to the Company. By 1801, the Company became the Overlord of Delhi. The Mughal Emperor became a pensioner of the Company. Shah Allam II died in Red Fort in 1806.

In 1813, the British Parliament brought out the Charter that observed that "Not only the profit but promotion of economic and technical aspect of Great Britain must be the objective of East India Company". Thus India became an open market for British goods and Indian goods were exported to U.K. on cheaper terms. The Charter also mentioned that an "Amount not less than one lakh rupees be spent on education of the natives, for the revival and improvement of literature and for promotion of science". In the above Charter it was not clear whether the amount was to be spent solely on promotion of the indigenous knowledge or on promotion of science education. Many people were in favour of the first option.

Along with the increase of power of East India Company, missionary activities also increased. In Calcutta, Madras and Bombay missionaries undertook projects to expand education. Book Society of Madras established in 1819 promoted Anglo-Vernacular Schools. And so also in Bengal and Bombay presidencies.

Lord T.B. Macaulay (1800-1859) came to India, reaching Madras on 10th June 1835. He was then 35 years of age and his income in England was mainly from his writings. When he got the offer to visit India on an assignment for 5 years, he was greatly delighted on this offer as it offered him both power and pelf. He wrote a letter to his sister saying, "He will earn £10,000 a year spending £4,000 and living like a prince. He will save £30,000" (*Jhunjhunwala* 2006 p. 37).

Macaulay chaired the Committee of Public Instruction. Many members of the Committee were of the view that the stipulated amount be spent on revival and improvement of indigenous (native) literature. Macaulay drastically disagreed in his Minutes of 2nd February 1835, be observed:

- We are not fettered by the pledge, expressed or implied, in the Act of Parliament 1813. We are free to employ our funds as we choose, that we ought to employ them in teaching which is best worth knowing, that English is better worth knowing than Sanskrit or Arabic, that natives were desirous to be taught English.

When we go critically in the text of the Minutes, we unearth Macaulay's perceptions:

- No amount be spent on improving native knowledge.
- Indigenous knowledge through Sanskrit or Arabic need not be promoted.
- Indigenous (native) literature is poor, inadequate and faulty. One single self of European library is worth the whole of native literature of India and Arabia.
- Education ought to be in English. Natives want it. It ought to be selective class-based, not mass-based.

- Aim of education at present must be, **to form a class of persons Indian in blood and colour but English in taste, opinion, morals and intellect.**
- Education will remain neutral to religion and culture.

Macaulay submitted his Minutes to the Governor General, Lord William Bentinck with the concluding para.

"If the decision of his Lordship should be such as I anticipate, I shall enter on the performance of my duties with the greatest zeal and alacrity. If, on the other hand, it be the opinion of Government that the present system ought to remain unchanged, I beg that I may be permitted to retire from the Chair of the Committee."

The Minutes were approved by the Governor General with following specifications:

- All funds be best employed on English Education alone imparting to Indians, a knowledge of English literature and science.
- Funds will not be spent on printing of oriental works.

5.3 A Peep into the mind of Macaulay

Some details about Macaulay's personality may help us to know the working of his mind. From the childhood, Macaulay was closely associated with Christian Missionaries especially with Willium Wilber Force who happened to be a close friend of his father and who saw all religions inferior to Christianity. In one of his letter to his father Macaulaty wrote (*Jhunjhunwala* 2006 p. 38), "English schools are progressing well. The demand of English Education is increasing to such an extent that we have not been able to admit willing students. In Hug city, 1400 students are learning English. This education will make significant impression on Hindus. After English Education, no Hindu will be fully dedicated to his religion.... It is my firm belief that after 30 years no idol worshipper will remain in Bengal if my education policy is followed rightly."

Macaulay also observed that India has wealth and high moral values. He was, therefore, inwardly resolved that this country cannot be conquered unless they break the backbone of this nation, which is her spiritual and cultural heritage. Thus he made curriculum totally anglo-centric devoid of national identity.

Macaulay's system of education, consciously and mindfully introduced five critical things:

- English as the medium of instruction from class one.
- Curriculum was totally anglo-centric, totally based on western history, geography, sciences and technologies.
- Total disregard to personality development, character development, value orientation.
- Zero space for vocation and work education.
- Total disregard to Indian culture, Indian identity and Indian ethos.

> *"It is impossible for us, with our limited means to attempt to educate the body of people. We may at present do our best to form a class who may be interpreters between us and the millions we govern."*
>
> *T.B. Macaulay*
> *2nd February, 1835*

5.4 Post Macaulay Reactions

English Education created suspicion and doubt in the minds of Bengalis, that it was an attempt to convert Hindus and Muslims to Christianity. Lord Bentinck allayed their fears reassuring that education will remain neutral to religious teaching. The undercurrent of dissatisfaction compelled the Government to set review and revisit educational policy. Thus came, **Wood's Educational Despatch of 1854**. It made clear that indigenous languages have their own importance and attempt must be made for mass education. But nothing substantial on the ground happened.

Narrulah and Naik (1951 p. 559), have observed that schools that came up during (1850-1880) could not do much except to correct a few blemishes of the official system. These schools never showed signs of an uncompromising revolt against the Government. Steele and Taylor (1994) also observed that education of the masses, importance of Indian languages and inclusion of work (vocational), education remained invisible and unrealized.

5.5 Educational Policy Initiatives (1854-1920)

Let us have a quick glance at the policy initiatives of Indian education (1854-1920):

Woods Educational Despatch Establishing Universities	1854 1857	• Vernaculars have their own importance. • Mass education is also government's responsibility. Three Universities were set up in Calcutta, Madras, Bombay.
Indian Education Commission Lord Curzon's Educational Policy (Government of India Resolution)	1882-83 1905	• Use of the mother tongue has its importance. • Education needs to be expanded and diversified. • Teacher education programmes may be initiated for primary and secondary teachers. • Private schools must satisfy conditions to receive Government's grant-in-aid. • Primary teachers must be trained in elementary agriculture.
Calcutta University Commission, Chair Dr. Sadler	1917-19	• Universities must have Department of Education. Education must be a subject in B.A. and M.A. degree exam.

Soon after Gandhiji's arrival in India, he was asked to speak on 6th February 1916 at the Banaras Hindu University establishment function. He was brave and bold to say, "It is a matter of humiliation and shame for us that I am compelled this evening in this sacred city to address my countrymen in a language foreign to me". He caught the pulse that one of the reasons of India's slavery is that our mother tongue is not given relevance. Before Gandhiji, Ishwar Chandra Vidyasagar, Swami Dayananda

Saraswati and R.N. Tagore had made massive contribution to give respect to the use of the mother tongue in education. But it was Gandhiji who proclaimed among prominent Englishmen and Rajas and Maharajas of India that to speak in English to our countrymen was a matter of shame and humiliation.

5.6 Prescribes Partial Remedy

Gandhiji's views on education in India (1920-1937) were based on his own innate reflections. Like deschoolers (Illitch. 1970 & Reimer 1971), he saw the futility of institutional learning. Like Paulo Freire (1970), the Brazilian educator, he wanted students to be aware of sociocultural reality and not to passively accept oppression but to resist the evil with non-violent means. Without using the words, 'radicalization', 'activization' and 'conscientization' he meant them all. He said, "Don't receive miseducation, leave it". In his concept of adult education and continuous education he foresaw Hutchins (1970) and Husen (1974).

When a national educational system gets vitiated, there can be two approaches for its amelioration. One to set up institution to provide the needed education. Second, to uproot the system and design a new one. The first approach is that of reformation substitution, the second is that of revolutionary revolt. Approaches undertaken by good schools set up by reformative India provided value-education and national identity. The approach by Gandhiji of 1920s was that of reformative substitution but the one given in 1937, the Nai Taleem, was revolutionary revolt. It was a step to create a silent social revolution, to develop rural esteem, to encourage production, to reduce poverty and to minimize rural to urban migration.

It was this undercurrent of thought that compelled Gandhiji to advise students to leave schools and colleges; and not to receive miseducation. Gandhiji's plea was triple boycott — English cloth, English courts and English educational institutions. Many students withdrew. Left colleges and schools and started participating in non-cooperation movement. Vidyapeeths were set up to provide national education in Gujarat, Bihar and U.P.

Vidyapeeths: With Gandhiji's call to students to leave citadels of slavery, Vidyapeeths were established in Ahmedabad, Banaras, Patna and Aligarh. Dr. Zakir Hussain, along with a group of national Muslims founded Jamia Islamia at Aligarh on 29th October, 1920. Before this Dr. Zakir Hussain wrote an inspirational article criticizing earlier role of Anglo Mohamedian Oriented College (AMO), Aligarh, set up under the leadership of Sir Syed Ahmed Khan (1817-1898). Dr. Zakir Hussain wanted Aligarh Muslim University to severe ties with Government and contribute to national resurgence. He strongly felt along with Gandhiji that national institutions need not be a machine of producing skilful subordinates for government offices. This institution, Jamia Islamia, was later on transferred to Delhi in August 1925. Gujarat Vidyapeeth was inaugurated on 15th November 1920. Speaking on this occasion Gandhiji said to students:

> *"You have undertaken to secure freedom through the miracle not of learning but of character, secure it not by meeting the Government sword against its shining sword but with peaceful spiritual effect... I have given the mantra. I fulfilled the function of a rishi if a vanik putra can do so".*

It has been observed (Nurullah and Naik 1951, p. 570), that nearly over a thousand alternative national schools came up by 1922. These institutions faced two problems, financial and stiff resistance from the Government Education Department. Inspite of these problems, followers of Gandhiji believed in boycotting government educational institutions. In *Young India* (24 June, 1921), Gandhiji said:

> *"I can see nothing wrong in the children, from the very threshold of their education paying for it in work. The simplest handicraft suitable for all, required for the whole of India is, undoubtedly spinning along with the previous processes. If we introduce this in our educational institutions, we should fulfil three purposes: make education self-sufficient, train the bodies of the children as well as their minds and pave the way for a complete boycott of foreign yarn and cloth."*

We can clearly see the seeds of Nai Taleem in the above statement. It has two elements; it takes a step towards making education self-sufficient (paying fee through work). It was also a step towards development of body and mind. Gandhiji's thinking gets reflected in two quotes:

- *"Man is neither mere intellect nor the gross animal body, nor the heart or soul alone. A proper and harmonious development of all the three is required for the making of the man and constitutes the true economics of education" (Harijan, 8 May, 1937).*
- *By education I mean all round drawing out the best in the child and man – body, mind and spirit (Harijan, 31 July, 1937).*

5.7 Dignity of Labour

As we shall see in the next chapter that one of the strands of Nai Taleem is productive work. This aspect caught Gandhiji's attention in 1919 with his love for Khadi. He advised one and all to abjure foreign cloth and wear home spin khadi. Spinning and weaving became his passion. R.N. Tagore disapproved Gandhiji's advice to spin and weave, and also to burn foreign clothes. During non-violent, non-Cooperation (Movement 1919-20), Gandhiji gave a call to leave British cloth, leave British Legal System and British Education System. His triple call was not appreciated by Sri Tagore, who was Gandhiji's warmest well-wisher and friend. Gandhiji always gave him the high status of "great guru". Tagore strongly disagreed that all children and adults must spin and help in production of local cloth. He published an article in the *Modern Review* under the title, "The Call of Truth". Before criticizing the idea, Tagore used the warmest words for Gandhiji (Bhattacharya 2001, pp. 68-87). (We repeat below expressions of both Tagore and Gandhiji).

> … At this juncture Mahatma Gandhi came and stood at the cottage door of the destitute millions clad as one of themselves… He has given us a vision of *shakti*, truth, for which our gratitude is unbounded. When we read about Truth

in books, we talk about it but it is indeed a **red-letter day** when we see it face-to-face. Rare is the moment in many a long year when such good fortune happen. For our master, the Mahatma may our devotion to him never grow less. We must learn the truth of love in all its purity but the science of building Swaraj is a vast subject. But he came to one narrow field. To one and all he simply says, "Spin and weave, spin and weave".

Gandhiji's reply to his "Gurudev" (respected teacher) was most warm, respectful and critical. It was full of courtesy, devotion and logic. It appeared in *Young India* of 13 October 1921. Gandhiji began his letter thus:

"The bard of Shantiniketan has contributed to the Modern Review a brilliant essays on the present movement. It is a series of word picture which alone he can paint. It is an eloquent protest against authority, slave mentality or whatever description one gives of blind acceptance of a passive mania. The poet tells summarily to reject each and everything that does not appeal to our reason and heart."

Gandhiji then very critically and logically writes why he is against foreign cloth and why he favours spinning wheel. He says that he has come to believe the spinning as the giver of plenty after a laborious thinking and great hesitation. Then he writes:

"He must not mistake the surface dust for the substance beneath. .... A plea for the spinning wheel is a plea for recognizing the dignity of labour. It was our love for foreign cloth that ousted the wheel from its position of dignity. Therefore, I consider it a sin to wear foreign cloth."

Gandhiji then quotes Verses from the Gita appealing not to eat without putting in labour. He builds the argument that the hungry millions in India ask for food. They must earn it. And they can earn only by the sweat of their brow. Spinning wheel is the answer. The trend that we note in 1921 became a powerful element of Basic Education of 1937.

5.8 Constructive Programmes

The holistic approach of Gandhiji was, "Oppose ill activities, promote healthy activities". He considered English Education as unhealthy education, miseducation and negative education. It was the duty of students to abjure this miseducation and indulge in educational activities that make the nation strong and united. He conceived about 20 activities that must be pursued with energy, enthusiasm and imagination. These activities were also to help India secure Swaraj. They were termed as constructive programmes, nearly 20 in number. We will cluster some under three categories for our understanding:

One

- Communal unity.
- Removal of untouchability.
- Uplifting downtrodden and marginalised, giving them dignity, individuality, respect and self-esteem.
- Promoting prohibition of use of alcohol and opium. Here Gandhiji followed one of the five percepts of Buddhism that includes "Non-drinking of alcohol".
- Use of Khadi a sure step to promote *swadeshi*, self-help, simplicity and dignity of labour.
- Promoting village industries, cottage industries and village development.
- Village sanitation.

Two

- Promoting Basic Education.
- Adult education.
- Education about health and hygiene.
- Promoting regional languages.
- Promoting all India link-language which is spoken by a large number of people.

Three

- Working for economic equality.
- Promoting social welfare of peasants, women, students and Adivasis.
- Special efforts to help leapers
- Special efforts to secure cow protection.

Gandhiji's faith in constructive programmes was immense. He advised Congress leadership to engage themselves with constructive programmes; thus becoming real servants of the society. In a letter written to Khan Abdul Gaffar Khan on 18 September 1942 Gandhiji writes, *"A non-violent man has to keep himself engaged usefully during all working hours in constructive work. Constructive work, therefore for him, is what arms are for the violent men"* (Iyer p. 252).

□

Three:

[illegible] economic capacity

- [illegible]
- [illegible] to help leaders
- Special efforts to [illegible]

[illegible]

[illegible] in constructing [illegible]

6

Nai Taleem: Background and Concept

- *"The artificial education that they could have had in England or South Africa torn from me would never have taught them simplicity and the spirit of service."*

  (Autob. p. 184)
- *"I had always given the first place to the culture of the heart or the building of character."*

  (Autob. p. 306)
- *"I merely gave the mantra, I fulfilled the function of a rishi if a vanik putra can do so."*

  (Inaugural speech at the setting up of Gujarat Vidyapeeth, 15 Nov., 1920)

6.1 Starter

We may recall that education, before the English system of education started in 1835, was community supported, had ethical and vocational edge. Each village had school run in teacher's own home or in a temple or mosque and the community bore financial burden. After 1835, English education was offered only for a selected few and had no ethical and vocational contents. This overall picture was greatly resisted. Gandhiji saw main dangers such as:

- Its unrootedness that did not develop individual identity.

- Its disconnect with moral and personal ethics and character building.
- Its disconnect with work education.
- Its disconnect with community service or social relationship.
- Its disregard to local language or mother tongue.

The main shift between Gandhiji views of 1937 and his earlier views was that he considered work education or vocational education as an important component of general education. In 1937, he realized that work education can be the foundation stone of education that cognitive development can depend on skill development.

6.2 Political Scenario

For understanding Basic Education or Nai Taleem, we need first to look at the political scenario. The First World War started in 1914. Lokmanya Bal Gangadhar Tilak returned from Mandala Jail (in Burma) in 1914. Gandhiji came to India in 1915. The Viceroy, Lord Chelmsford, invited him to the Conference to support the resolution about recruiting. He said, "With a full sense of my responsibility, I beg to support the resolution (Autob. p. 408). Gandhiji inspite of his love for non-violence undertook the task of recruitment of Indians for the war. This activity made him severely sick."

After the war the British Government passed the Government of India Act 1919 which aimed to provide increasing association of Indians in administration to gradually develop self-governing institutions. This Act was known as Diarchy, a two-tier system of Executive Councils. The elected Indian executive members were to preside over transferred departments (such as education) and the Indians appointed by the Governor, to rule over reserved departments, which included finance and law and order. Thus Indians (elected executive members), were given the chance to reform and re-organise education as they saw fit. But this dream remained a dream and could not be materialized.

Jalianawala Bagh massacre of 13 April, 1919, and later on promulgation of Rowlatt's Bill made Gandhiji to stand against the British Raj. He pleaded for triple boycott, British Courts, British Cloth and Government schools and colleges. This appeal was the basis of establishing Vidyapeeths in 1920s.

Government of India Act, 1935: Due to non-cooperation movement, the Diarchy system of 1919 massively failed to reform and restructure education. It also failed to make education a mass movement for one and all students between 6 to 14. The Government of India Act 1935, provided Provincial Autonomy. After Provincial elections of 1937, Congress came into power and formed government in the most of the provinces. Through Harijan, Gandhiji made radical proposal to Congress Ministers. He wanted the Ministers to lead a simple life, not to copy the British officials, to promote prohibition, to reform jails, to use Khadi, and to make Salt free for all. Among these reforms was the suggestion for mass education. In 1937, he focused his full attention to mass education of seven years, from the age of 7 to 14.

Leadership of Gandhiji was very unique. He practiced what he preached. For him knowing was being. In his life practice and precepts went hand-in-hand. For him education was not imparting of facts or concepts but to acquire a mindset or pattern of behaviour. Let us look at the first public meeting of Gandhiji (in 1894), in Pretoria in the house of Mohammad Haji Joosab to orient Indians what they ought to do. He highlighted some points where we see a true teacher in him. He was to lead and enthuse others to work. He said:

- "Our responsibility to be truthful was all the greater in a foreignland."
- "Our people have habits of insanitation as compared to Englishmen around them."
- "We often divide ourselves into Madrasi or Punjabi or Hindu or Muslim. We ought to forget this distinction."

Gandhiji also suggested that there ought to be an association that will represent hardships and problems faced by Indians to the authorities. As, many Indians were not knowing English, he offered himself as a teacher to those who would like to learn English. This spirit of a true teacher which was tacit in 1894 came up in full force in 1937. Before we look at Gandhiji's educational vision, we first need to peep into what he called as his, "educational fads".

6.3 Educational Fads

Learning English which Gandhiji saw as a student in Rajkot greatly distressed him. He sincerely felt that foreign medium put an undue stress on students. It kills original thought, makes students crammers and imitators. It makes children foreigners in their own land. Teaching in English in India, in colleges and universities continued indirectly till 1947 with the result that it stunted the growth of vernaculars.

Teachers and students who read closely two works of Gandhiji namely his Autobiography and *Hind Swaraj*, will find many comments that speak of Gandhiji's thoughts on education. Here, we focus on four occasions. One of 1897 when he landed at Durban with three children, he did not put them in any European School, nor kept English teacher but decided to teach them himself. It is true that he could not devote full time to them but by keeping these children with him he taught them "Simplicity and the spirit of service".

Belittling one's mother tongue is like disparaging one's own mother.

The second one relates to 1910 when he devoted his full time to teach students on health, character, literacy and work. In his (Autob. p. 306-312), Gandhiji devotes four chapters: *As school teacher, literary training, training of the spirit and tares among the wheat.* Each chapter contains deep contents that led him to take two important decisions in 1919-20 and in 1937; the first relating to asking children to withdrawn from schools and colleges and the second one relates to *Buniyadi Shiksha* or Nai Taleem.

The third one relates to his visit to Shantiniketan in 1915 (pp. 349-351). His Phoenix team was there and he quickly mixed with teachers and students and suggested them to do away with the paid cooks and manage their own kitchen. It was an experiment in simplicity and self-help. Batches were formed to cut vegetables, to clean the grain and cleaning kitchen and its surroundings. Phoenix party kitchen was totally self-managed, supervised by Magan Lal Gandhi, and the food cooked was the simplest, "Condiments were eschewed. Rice, dal, vegetables and even wheat-flour were all cooked at one and the same time in a steam cooker. The experiment was, however, dropped after sometime." Tagore said to his boys, "The experiment contains the key to Swaraj" (Autob. p. 351).

The fourth one relates to starting schools in Bihar when his work on *Tinkathie* system was going on. Gandhiji writes (Autob. p. 386), "I decided to open primary schools in six villages. Villages agreed to provide foodgrain but the problem was to get the good teachers". Again he started from his own end. His wife Kasturbai, his son Devdas, Mahadeo Desai and a few others came. The emphasis was more on teaching cleanliness and good manner than teaching grammar or three Rs. Doctors were also needed and Dr. Dev from the Servants of India Society, Pune came. With the school work, classes for women and adults also were started.

6.4 Gandhi on Basic Education

The term 'basic', may cause a bit of confusion to readers especially to the west. It was used by Mahatma Gandhiji in 1937. It has also been used by UNESCO in 70s. It was again used by UN agencies in 1990. It is good to look at this term from different perspectives, as it connotes different meaning in different context.

Gandhiji used terms like primary education or elementary education in *Hind Swaraj*. He had said a few things that lead to the idea of basic education which he later on called Nai Taleem or *Buniyadi Shiksha* or Basic Education in 1937. In his view primary education ought to develop discontent with injustice and cooperation with justice. As O.A. Hume thought that the Congress should spread discontent in Indians, so also education must develop cooperation with good and non-cooperation with evil. Dadabhai Naoroji said that education has opened our eyes to "UnBritish rule in India that had sucked our lifeblood." Education must feed us patience. Education must teach us not to be sycophant but to be objective, analytical and truthful. "The English has not taken India, we have given it to them". Education must make us fearless. Strength lies in absence of fear. These were the "Educational fads", of Gandhiji.

Hind Swaraj makes this point over and over again. Education must prepare the country for the faculty of assimilation especially for Hindu-Muslim Unity. "If everyone will try to understand the core of his own religion and adhere to it and will not allow false teachers to dictate, there will be no room left for quarrelling". Religious, or ethical education, must occupy the first place. Gandhiji in *Hind Swaraj* does not totally decry knowledge of letters, he decisively makes a point that elementary education or higher education does not help in, "Controlling senses" that "It does not make man of us". It "Does not enable us to do our duty". In his view "Character building has the first place in it and that is primary education". These aspects are implicitly covered when Gandhiji uses the term, "Basic Education".

6.5 UNESCO's Concept

UNESCO (Coombs et al. 1973), uses the term basic education that includes:

- Literacy and numeracy.
- Elementary understanding of society and nature.
- Positive attitude towards work, family and community.
- Scientific outlook, spirit of cooperation and tolerance.
- Foundation skills for earning and living.
- Foundational skills and Knowledge of Citizenship

In 1990, UN Agencies, UNDP, UNESCO and others, at Jomtien, gave the call of, **Education for All** (EFA). It was adopted in India as *Sarva Shiksha Abhiyan* (SSA).

Efforts towards mass education in India started as early as in 1911 but failed. Sri Gopal Krishna Gokhale moved a proposal for mass education but it was not accepted. Later on in 1937 Gandhiji gave a call of Nai Taleem; compulsory mass education in mother tongue for children of 7 to 14. It made some impact but could not become an all India venture. When India became free in 1947 the educational picture was a dismal one. Literacy 32% and enrolment in primary classes about 45% with huge withdrawal by Class V.

6.6 Basic Education: A Passport to Life

UNESCO (1996 p. 118), looks at basic education as a passport for life. It defines it as "Initial education (formal and non-formal), extending from 3 to at least age 12. It enables people to choose what they do to share in building the collective future and to continue to learn. It also brings out another important point. It must make good the knowledge deficit that is closely linked to underdevelopment. This report (Unesco 1996 p. 25), also reproduces basic learning needs as specified in the Jomtien World Conference on Education for All" (WCEFA 1990 para 1 Art. 1).

> *"These learning needs comprise both learning tools (such as literacy, oral expression, numeracy and problem solving), and the basic learning content (such as knowledge, skill, values, and attitudes), required by human beings to be able to survive to develop their work in dignity, to participate fully in development, to improve quality of their lives, to make informed decisions and to continue to learn."*

Dr. Karan Singh, as one of the members of International Commission, Unesco 1996, writes most forcefully in his article, "Education for the Global Society" (pp. 225-227), that inter-faith dialogue need special attention. "The spiritual dimension will have to be given central importance in our new educational thinking".

6.7 Understanding Vidya through Gandhiji's Lens

Concept of *Vidya* in Indian scriptures has two aspects *apara* and *para*: The first relates to the worldly knowledge (or what the Gita calls as knowledge of क्षेत्र) and the other relates to understanding The Brahman or The Truth or The Reality Character of the learner is the most important factor in knowing both the *apara* and *para vidya*. Swami Vivekananda, when he set up Ramakrishna Matha (on 1st May 1897), decided the motto as self-realisation as well as doing good in the world आत्मनो मोक्षार्थम् जगत हिताय च।

Gandhiji wanted education to awaken national consciousness and prepare students for truth and non-violence. He wanted education to prepare students who will oppose social unjustice and human inequality. He wanted education to work for social justice and human dignity. He wanted that education ought to develop a mindset to serve others without ego.

The concept of the Gita of *Loka Sangraha*, needs to be hermeneutically interpreted. It is a complex and broad concept that also includes relationship with the power group. If those in power adopt self-promoting and repressive policies then a thoughtful individual, call him a social activist, must oppose. In a letter to Tagore Gandhiji wrote, "Non-cooperation with evil is as much a duty, as cooperation with the good. Gandhiji did not object to liberal education. But his definition of education was very broad." As he says in *Hind Swaraj*, "A person can be an educated person without the knowledge of ₹ 3. For him good education must develop good habits and love for humanity. Developing habits of simplicity, hardwork and the spirit of service must be the main objectives of education."

If we want to understand Gandhiji's vision of education, especially relating to Basic Education, we need to understand his world-view. His world-view was an integrated whole with inter-twinned strands such as:

- Living and non-living are not separate entities. Both are the part of Brahman. The Gita (13.19) says प्रकृति पुरुष चैव विद्धि अनादी उभावति (Purusha and Prakriti both are eternal and interconnected). When Gandhiji was criticized in 1934, on his views on earthquakes, this was what he said to Tagore. "Education, economics, politics, technology and culture are all components of life. They cannot be divorced from spiritual aspect which must guide them and all life activities." He said, "I confess, I do not draw a sharp line or any distinction between economics and ethics."
- Villages are the places where India lives. They must be made self-contained, self-supportive, dynamic, vibrate and receptive.

- We must act to perform our duty which has its own reward. No action of Gandhiji can be understood if we do not understand, *"Ansakti yoga"*, which he draws from the Gita.
- "Means" and "ends" are not two entities. No good end can ever be activated by bad or evil means.
- Our actions must be more powerful than our words; that our speech must reflect our thoughts, that we must speak boldly what we feel, and not speak to please our political masters.
- Knowledge emerges out of our actions. The cognitive development in education must be the product of work and labour. In life our experience must teach us to see the truth as that is at a given moment.

All the above aspects must be considered vital to understand Gandhiji's vision of Basic Education. For him parents and the teacher are the main promoters of "Education of the spirit". Textbooks for him were the least important inputs in imparting education.

Gandhiji's eleven vows cannot be overlooked when we consider his educational vision. His emphasis on self-suffering, self-simplification, self-purification and living a life of voluntary poverty are indeed based on the first five vows which are called as *"yama"*. The next six vows (physical labour, respect to all religions, *swadeshi*, rejecting the notion of untouchability, fearlessness and eating not for the palate), are most relevant when he called basic education a silent social revolution promoting dignity of the poor and bridging the gap between the poor, rural and urban rich.

□

7
The Seed Germinates and Withers

- *"True education lies in serving others, oblige them without the least feeling one-uppishness."*

  (Letter to Ramdas Gandhi)
- *"To do good to others and serve them without any sense of egoism that is real education."*

  (Letter to Manilal Gandhi)
- *"That action is better than speech; that it is our duty to say exactly what we think and face the consequences and only then that we shall be able to impress anybody with our speech."*

  (Hind Swaraj, p. 91)

7.1 Starter

Gandhiji, since 1897, had been an active thinker on education. He saw it both as means and as an end. He saw the intrinsic qualities as well as the instrumental qualities of education. His call to leave government schools and colleges in 1919-20 was based on the fact that education that was being imparted to students was no education. The mother tongue of the student was not used, educational curricula was anglo-centric. No attempt was done to develop character of students. National identity, nationalism, patriotism were never the content of learning.

7.2 The Wardha Conference

Gandhiji's life was multi-dimensional. He was busy in the removal of, "UnBritish", rule in India, in strengthening the concept of Swaraj, in promoting Hindu-Muslim Unity, in removal of untouchability and in promoting village development. During 1935 to 1937 he thought actively and came up with a scheme which he called as Nai Taleem or Basic Education or "Buniyadi Shiksha." He thought holistically and organically on all aspects of education.

> *Fie on modern education... Getting by heart the thought of others in a foreign language and stuffing your brain with them and taking some university degree. You consider yourself educated. Is this education?*
>
> *Swami Vivekanand*

His idea coincides and merges with Swami Vivekanand who considered education as a man making and national building activity. Stuffing brain with information often with useless details and not building moral aspect of the student's life was no education. Gandhiji came up with basic bricks of Nai Taleem but he wanted educationist of the day to reflect on his educational scheme thoughtfully and suggest any modification, if needed.

It was decided that Conference may be convened on 22 and 23 October 1937 of nationally minded educationists to reflect and discuss Gandhiji's idea on education. Later on this Conference was called as *Wardha Conference.*

As we had mentioned Gandhiji wanted silent social revolution through education. Education has to have non-violence, truth and self-sufficiency through work, at its base. Gandhiji, himself, presided over the Wardha Conference. Only one brave note of dissent was from Prof. K.T. Shah. Most of the participants of the Conference (nearly 80) supported it. Four recommendations that came out of the Conference were:

- Free and compulsory education be provided for seven years on a nationwide scale.
- The medium of instruction be the mother tongue.
- The process of education should centre around same form of manual and productive work; all educational activities

should be integrally related to handicraft with due regard to child's environment.

- The system of education will be gradually able to cover the remuneration of the teacher.

When we look critically at the above four resolutions we miss the Gandhiji's tone and spirit.

(a) Self-sufficiency.

(b) Silent social revolution to build self-esteem of the village learner and bridging the economic gap between poor rural and urban rich people.

(c) Non-violence and Truth must become integral part of Nai Taleem to inculcate self-simplification and self-purification needed for ethically centred life.

After the conference it was decided that a committee be appointed to work out syllabus and train teachers. Dr. Zakir Hussain was to be the Chairman. He worked out the scheme which was to have three focal points of co-relation:

- Educational activity and the craft work.
- Educational activity and physical environment.
- Educational activity and social environment.

In the Haripur Session, Congress governments adopted Basic Education as their main agenda. But for most of Congress Education Ministers it was free and compulsory education on a nationwide scale through the mother tongue around a craft appropriate to child's physical surrounding. The concept of silent social revolution, enhancing the self-esteem of the people of rural area, demanding drastic life simplification and purification and financial self-dependency were the unknown and alien words. The spirit of Gandhiji could not percolate in the recommendations of the Wardha Scheme, nor in the minds of school authorities who were managing Nai Taleem or Model Basic Schools.

7.3 Polarization of Perspectives

Education was seen by Gandhiji as training in morality, in developing life simplification, helping both teachers and students to lead severely simple life by drastically reducing needs and desires. It aimed at developing village and cottage industries. This type of education will stand in opposition to the developmental model that supports industrialization, urbanization, modernization and competition. One model of development was based on inner moral transformation demanding self-purity, self-suffering, self-simplicity by self-imposed restrictions. Another model was based on scientific rationalistic, socialistic thinking needed to live in modern industralised world that demands competition. The second perspective demanded economic planning carried out by a strong centralized body. This perception had an ambitious agenda of industrialization. The other perspective, the Gandhian perspective was based on no faith on modernization and industrialization as it was a Seven Day Wonder. It kills human worth, human dignity and joy of working with hands. The Gandhian model of development was based on to make the poorest and the weakest happy, it was meant to remove tears from his eyes and to restore him to control his own destiny. The model of industrialization had the backing of Pt. Nehru. And the majority was with him.

7.4 The Seed Germinates

The seed of Basic Education, germinated and grew. We see three factors; one the force of the personality of Gandhiji, two, the force inherent in the idea itself which some (not many) people appreciated, three, due to the sincerity and tenacity of the person (Dr. Zakir Hussain) who was put as the Chairman of Conference of Nai Taleem.

(i) **Strength of Gandhiji's Personality** – The most important factor behind acceptance of Nai Taleem in India was the personality of Gandhiji. For the most of Indians he was indeed a great soul, the Mahatma, "Made of a different clay", as observed by Nehru, "His deeds were more powerful than his words", as observed by Tagore. Those who didn't like him or opposed him politically and economically and who called him, "muddle headed" a, "cunning *bania*", "an irrelevant old fool" never doubted his nationalism, patriotism, idealism and honesty. As a person he had the mass appeal. Anything that came from him was respected and accepted.

(ii) **Strength of the innate idea of** Nai Taleem – After 1911, Gandhiji was the first person to take up the question of mass education, nationwide for children of seven to fourteen. It was a seven year educational programme through the use of the mother tongue. It opposed teaching through English. Those who were on the same wavelength of Gandhi also understood immense important role of education for character building and leading a simple, pure life voluntarily reducing needs and desires. Thus those who wholeheartedly accepted the idea of Nai Taleem like Kaka Kalelkar and Vinoba Bhave saw it as a revolutionary alternative to government-run-educational activity.

(iii) **Deep Commitment of Dr. Zakir Hussain** – The third factor that led the seed to germinate and to become a sapling was the competence and commitment of the Chairman, Nai Taleem, Dr. Zakir Hussain. After Wardha Conference, Gandhiji appointed him as the Chairman of Nai Taleem. Dr. Zakir Hussain's German experience had given him first-hand knowledge of Work Schools of Germany. He was considered as world-class educationist both by Hindus and Muslims. His informal and unassuming personality was the factor that made Basic Education acceptable to Central Advisory Board of Education (CABE).

7.5 Sapling Withers

Political changes that came with Government of India Act 1935 became weak and uncertain due to World War II. After 1939, all efforts in India and England were to strengthen defence capabilities. The "Quit India" movement of 1942 stood opposed to defence preparations. These activities naturally weakened the spirit and activities of Nai Taleem. Besides the above "seen" and "tangible" reasons, there were some unseen and intangible reasons, we see three:

- Except a few honourable exception the spirit of Gandhiji's Basic Education was not understood by many educationists (They understood the word not the spirit).
- Whatever was understood needed massive preparation especially in three areas of Design of curriculum, Training of teachers and Developing study materials.
- Whatever done in the area of curriculum design, teacher training and development of study materials, was totally inadequate to make this scheme operative on the nation-wide scale. Work was done in all the above areas but was done at few locations only like Jamia Milia and Gujarat Vidyapeeth.

7.6 Zakir Sahib's Special Efforts

One agrees with the observations of Salamatullah and Qudri (1999 p. 10) that Zakir Sahib "Turned Gandhiji's concept of Basic Education, an uncut diamond, into Koh-i-noor". As a person Zakir Sahib was greatly influenced by Gandhiji. He desired, in 1920, that Aligarh Muslim University, must severe its connection with the Government and prepare students for national aspirations. With his German experience, he was one with Gandhiji. While in Germany he visited Work Schools which considered work as educative producing higher values of life and not merely meeting personal ends. Work Schools did not discard liberal education but gave prominence to cultural heritage which Dr. Zakir Hussain refers as **cultural goods** that is; cooperation, initiative individual responsibility, planning of details, etc.

The Wardha Conference, presided by Gandhiji appointed a Committee of ten members with Dr. Zakir Hussain as the Chairperson. Nonetheless the Central Advisory Board of Education (CABE) wanted to examine the details and ramifications of Nai Taleem. CABE, thus constituted a committee under B.G. Kher in 1938, to look into all aspects of Basic Education. Dr. Zakir Hussain was also a member of this Committee. Most of the members of the Committee considered Basic Education as a production rather than an educational scheme. Muslim League rejected Nai Taleem as it involved inculcation of non-violence as a part of it. Dr. Zakir Hussain had the hard task to convince both the CABE and the Muslim League on the merits of Basic Education. With his untiring efforts he made parties and the CABE to agree on:

- Education through mother tongue.
- Education over a period of seven years.
- Education to be organized around useful productive work.

When the Second World War started in 1939 and Government concentrated on securing war support, Congress ministers in provinces resigned. This was a great setback to the Nai Taleem. The Second Basic Education Conference was held in 1941. Zakir Sahib observed in his Presidential address that work of Basic Education must go on with or without government help. But the superfluous implementation of Basic Education made Zakir Sahib resign and dissociate himself from *Hindusthan Taleemi Sangha* in 1948. For broader awareness the names of members of the Zakir Hussain Committee are given below:

MEMBERS OF THE ZAKIR HUSSAIN COMMITTEE

That the Committee was composed of persons competent to speak on the subject of education is apparent from the educational qualifications and experience of the members.

Dr. Zakir Hussain, had his education in Germany, is a Ph.D. of Berlin University, is a German Scholar and has been in-charge of the Jamia Millia Islamia ever since its inception. He has thus considerable experience of primary and higher education both.

Prof. Khwaja Saiyidain, belongs to the Aligarh University and is B.A., M.Ed. (Leeds).

Shri Vinoba, has no academic qualifications, but is known for his profound learning and has had educational experience extending over 20 years.

Shri Kakasaheb Kalelkar, is a graduate of the Bombay University, has been an educationist all his life, having taught at

Shantiniketan, Satyagrahashram School, Sabarmati and Gujarat Vidyapeeth of which he was Principal.

Shri Kishorlal Mashruwala, is a B.A., LL.B of Bombay University, taught at Satyagrahashram School, Sabarmati, and was Registrar and Professor of the Gujarat Vidyapeeth for many years. He has thought deeply on education and has several educational books to his credit.

Shrimati Ashadevi, is a double M.A. in English and Sanskrit of the Banaras Hindu University, and has the natural gift of teaching. She has been in-charge of the women's section in the Banaras University, and Mahila Vidyalaya, Wardha.

Shri Shrikrishna Jajuji, B.A., B.L. was Chairman of the Managing Board of the A.I.V.I.A. and has a fund of practical experience of handicrafts, having also been long associated with the A.I. Spinners' Association.

Prof. K.T. Shah, B.A. (Bombay), B.Sc. (London), Bar-at-Law, has had much to do with University education for many years, is the author of numerous books on Economics, and was a member of the Debt Inquiry Committee appointed by the Congress.

Smt. J.C. Kumarappa, is M.A. (Columbia), B.Sc. (Syracuse), and is an Incorporate Accountant. He abandoned a lucrative career as Accountant in 1929 and joined the Gujarat Vidyapeeth as Professor of Economics, carried out an economic survey of Matar Taluka in Gujarat, was on the Public Debt Inquiry Committee appointed by the Congress, and has been the Secretary of the A.I.V.I.A. ever since its inception.

Shri Aryanayakam, had his training abroad, and is B.D., B.Ed. (Hons.) (Edin.), Diploma in Education (Cantab), F.R.S.A. He was for long in Shantiniketan and is now Principal of Navbharat Vidyalaya, Wardha.

□

Shantiniketan [illegible] School, [illegible] and [illegible] Vidyapeeth of which he was Principal.

[illegible]

Registrar and Professor of the University [illegible] for many years [illegible]

[illegible]

[illegible] by him [illegible]

[illegible] Shantiniketan and is now [illegible]

8
Paradigm for Re-engineering

- *The world we leave to our children depend on the children we leave to the world.*

  World Education Report 1998
- *The British administration when they came to India, instead of taking things as they were began to root them out. They scratched the soil and began to look at root and the beautiful tree parished. The village schools were not good enough for the British administrator so he came out with his programme.*

  M.K. Gandhi
  London, Round Table Conference 1931
- *Our education has got to be revolutionized. The brain must be educated through the hand.*

  M.K. Gandhi
  18 February 1938

8.1 Starter

Man is the only being who acts in the present keeping in view the experiences of the past as well as the aspiration and vision for the future. From 30th January 1948 to 2013, a lot was done and a lot was not done. Excellent decisions were taken and unwise, if not silly, decisions were also taken. The march of educational events moved but moved slowly. Many times the march was bold and adventurous, setting up IITs, IIMs and of rural institutes in 1956 onwards.

Establishing NCERT, setting up of DIETs, declaring minimum levels of learning, Operation Blackboard, etc. were wise steps. Many steps were dull, prosaic and negative. Closing down multipurpose schools, closing down training of vocational teachers, offering twin streams of academic and vocational education were unwise decisions.

To guess future, to use the Churchillian expression is, "A riddle wrapped in mystery inside an enigma". Education will suffer a huge loss if it leaves Gandhian views out of its context; which it has done, unfailingly, for the last 66 years.

International educational currents of deschooling society (lllitch 1970), School is Dead (Reimer 1971), made their impact. Then came educational technology, open schools, open universities and alternative strategies including non-formal education… Basic Education (Nai Taleem), was conspicuous by its absence. Impact of WCEFA, 1990, on India was launching of *Sarva Shiksha Abhiyan* in 2002. It was a wise step but lacked Gandhian Vision.

It was decided that, Right to Education (RTE) will be operationalised from 2002. It took seven years. The Act RTE-2009 has never mentioned a 'word' about Nai Taleem or work education or character formation. This is how our great thinkers think greatly.

8.2 Cultural Amnesia

It seems, educational policy-makers from 1947 to 2013, have forgotten cultural contents of education and the views of great Indian thinkers on education. After 30th January 1948, we ask ourselves, did we do anything to promote what Gandhiji called as silent social revolution; did we do anything to educate the brain through the hand; did we do anything to undertake continual spiritual evolution of the student, did we do anything to provide all-round development of intellect, body and spirit, did we make manual training, the principal means of stimulating intellect. To be honest to ourselves and to Gandhiji we did not do anything.

Basic education was put on the back burner. And we forgot that we have forgotten Nai Taleem.

The first Commission in free India was on University education. The second one was on Secondary education and the third one was on Education and National Development. No one in India from January 30, 1948 to 1966 thought about Basic Education. Again from 1966 to 2012 Government seems to be overlooking the concept of Basic Education. Even the, Right to Education 2009, seems indifferent to Basic Education.

Even the vocational education offered through multi-purpose schools came to a quick half. Training of vocational teachers was abandoned by NCERT-run-Regional Colleges of Education. Kothari Commission (1964-66), most surprisingly, made vocational stream a separate stream.

8.3 Right to Education: Essentials Missing

Before 15 August 1947, there were about 17 universities, 4000 high schools, 9000 middle schools and around 1,50,000 primary schools. Enrolment at the primary level was low and dismal. National decision to make mass education nationwide and to make education "A fundamental right", came in 2002. It took seven long years to become an Act, "The Right of Children to free and Compulsory Education Act, 2009" (No. 35 of 2009, dated 26 August 2009).

The Act, meticulously clear and specific, provides information on right to children to get admitted in a neighbouring school and seek transfer if needed. It provides in details duty of Centre and State governments, local authority and parents. The Act includes provision of, National Curriculum Framework and technical support to transact curriculum, it provides proper training of teachers and their duty, responsibilities of school and adhering to the academic calendar. The Act makes an excellent proposal to constitute School Management Committee to perform specific functions. There is a chapter on Protection of Rights of Children. The Act, thus, is indeed an excellent document on all administrative details. Academic aspects have also been touched but in a light and general way. **They lack critical rigour.** We list a few below:

- The Act does not indicate whether the curricula to be designed by the appropriate authority at the National and State levels will be "inclusive" or "sequential curriculum". The indication that one gets is: The curriculum is sequential because at present (by July 2013), the Curriculum followed at the national level is NCF 2005 which is essentially sequential. The RTE 2009 ought to have self-contained inclusive curriculum. Do we want 8 year free and compulsory education as a beginning part of secondary education or do we want it to be a self-contained inclusive period of education, which it ought to be.
- The second glaring omission is total absence of vocational training during this free and compulsory exposure of eight years of education. The child must develop foundation skills of work or a vocation to help him to earn his livelihood. Eight years of stay in a school is a long period and skills of one or two vocations must be initiated in this period. This aspect cannot be left to the authority designing national or state level curriculum. It is a policy issue and cannot be left to the wisdom or whims of members of Curriculum Designing Committee. Education of the hand cannot be left to the will of individuals.
- The third glorious omission is with respect to education of the heart. The Chapter V, under Section 29(2), mentions:
  (a) Conformity with values enshrined in the constitution.
  (b) All round development of the child.
  (c) Building up child's knowledge, potentiality and talent.

All the above specifications are general in nature. It would have been much better if the framers of the Act could have specifically mentioned values as given in Ten Fundamental Duties as given in 51A. Besides the Fundamental Duties, this author will also plead for inclusion of core aspect of Curriculum as given in National Policy on Education.

Fundamental Duties

Fundamental Duties — It shall be the duty of every citizen of India —

(a) To abide by the Constitution and respect its ideals and institutions, the National Flag and the National Anthem.

(b) To cherish and follow the noble ideals which inspired our national struggle for freedom.

(c) To uphold and protect the sovereignty, unity and integrity of India.

(d) To defend the country and render national service when called upon to do so.

(e) To promote harmony and the spirit of common brotherhood amongst all the people of India transcending religious, linguistic and regional or sectional diversities; to renounce practices derogatory to the dignity of women.

(f) To value and preserve the rich heritage of our composite culture.

(g) To protect and improve the natural environment including forests, lakes, rivers, wildlife and to have compassion for living creatures.

(h) To develop the scientific temper, humanism and the spirit of inquiry and reform.

(i) To safeguard public property and to abjure violence.

(j) To strive towards excellence in all spheres of individual and collective activity so that the nation constantly rises to higher levels of endeavour and achievement.

Core Aspects of Curriculum (as given in NPE 1986/92)

1. The history of India's freedom movement.
2. The Constitutional obligations.
3. Content essential to nurture national identity.
4. India's common cultural heritage.
5. Egalitarianism.
6. Democracy and secularism.
7. Equality of sexes.
8. Protection of environment.
9. Removal of social barriers.
10. Observation of small family norms and inculcation of scientific temper.

The initial eights years of education must develop in all learners national identity, healthy living habits, love to undertake sustained hard work, respect to national property, desire to live peacefully with others and a sense to resolve issues by dialogue, discussion and pursuation. If eight years of free and compulsory education cannot develop these personality traits, cognitive learning of four or five subjects is not a big achievement. These are the essentials that ought to have been mentioned in the Act; and, on which, the Act is silent.

8.4 Re-engineering Basic Education

If we have respect for Gandhiji and faith in his ideas, we need to bring back to life the educational dream of Gandhiji which he envisioned in *Nai Taleem* or *Buniyadi Shiksha*. And we can do it if we really wish it.

Nation may set up a new body National Council of Basic Education and Educational Innovations (NCBEEI). In each district a Model Basic School be set up to provide eight years of elementary education. It may have curriculum equivalent to CBSE but not similar. The school must be a fully residential school with enough land to cultivate and grow trees and fruit plants. It must have good networking with industrial houses and cottage industries to start vocational courses with multiple entry and exit points.

Along with cognitive learning of three Rs (reading, writing and arithmetic), it must involve all students on work education. Each student must be taught *life skills* that are most essential to all. This author will give a few examples:

- All students must be taught how to breath properly.
- All students must be exposed to those techniques that improves and enhances power of concentration and focused attention.
- All students must be trained in "Good listening"; listening with respect, attention and without pre-evaluation.
- All students must be oriented to speak such words which do not irritate others, do not make others furious. How to

speak kindly and truthfully is to be taught in special sessions.

The timetable of Nai Taleem Schools should be such that runs from 5 a.m. to 10.30 p.m. Cognitive learning could be grouped as follows:

Class 1,2 & 3	Basic 3 ₹ and life skills.
Class 4,5,6	Integrated and thematic science, social studies, maths, two languages, life skills and work experience.
Class 7, 8	Work experience, basic life skills and school subjects.

The (NCBEEI) should have separate Board and one training and management college at the national level to train teachers, Heads, Principals and Evaluators. This Council (NCBEEI) ought to have different rules for appointing Teachers, Heads of institutions that provide flexibility, openness and accountability. If the whole experiment cannot be launched on a nationwide scale at least Five Model Basic Schools be set up in different regions of India on a *pilot-project basis* for 5 years. We can relive Gandhiji's ideas if we have the will and boldness to act.

□

9

Epilogue

With this chapter we end this book. Gandhiji transformed himself and inspired others. He never worked as a teacher in any school although he very much wanted to do so. He did apply (Autob. p. 88), but he was not interviewed as he was not a graduate. With his egolessness and self-effacement, he struggled throughout his life to assert dignity of the individual and his autonomy. Being an astute *sanatani Hindu*, he opposed the degrading notion of untouchability, and respected all religions. He believed that we need to withdraw our support to the government if its acts harm the nation. Let us look closely at some of his sterling qualities.

Humility

Gandhiji, as a person, was never arrogant, haughty, boastful or pompous. When people talked of, "Gandhian ideology", he said in his own style. "I adore truth and non-violence. I try to live them in my life but many times I failed due to my own imperfections." Thus, he said, "World's praise fails to move me indeed it often stings me" (Autob. p. 464). When people praised him of introducing non-violence in public life and political dealings he said, "I have done nothing new. Truth and non-violence are as old as the hills".

Repentance

One is great if one recognizes one's mistakes and goes for public forgiveness. When the non-cooperation movement resulted into stray cases of violence and destruction of public property, he was bold enough to say that he has committed Himalayan Blunder and asked the Public to forgive him. It is rarely seen that people of national status declare openly that they have made a mistake and ought to be forgiven for their wrong decision. On the other hand when Lord Linlithgow impeached him of his policies which resulted into mass violence, he strongly refuted his argument and willed to crucify himself by taking a 21-day fast.

His sense of repentance was unique. On two different occasions he repented for the wrongs of others as he felt he was responsible in some measure for the wrongs of others. Two instances relate to fast described earlier, in 1910 for the wrong act of two individuals of Tolstoy Farm, and another for the dwindling support to hartal of Ahmedabad Mill Workers.

Positivity

Positivity was the hallmark of Gandhiji. His positivity can be seen when he advised Dada Abdulla & Co. to decide the case by arbitration and not to go to law court. Another aspect of his positivity was when he advised Dada Abdulla & Co. to accept payment in installments. His positive thinking can be seen when he pleaded with Lord Mountbatten not to divide the country but make Mr. Jinnah the Prime Minister of United India.

In 1931, when he visited London to attend Second Round Table Conference, he met the King Emperor. When the King asked him that it was reported that he (Gandhi), was busy in seditious activities, he most mildly said, "Your Majesty, I would not like to enter into argument with you." After the meeting when press asked him was he properly dressed for the meeting? He said, "The King had on enough for both of us." When Winston Churchill called him, "Half-naked *fakir*", he said, "I am grateful for the remark. I have still to go a long way to be a fully naked *fakir*."

Gandhiji always followed the principle that One who had heart to help can only offer criticism. In a letter written to Lord Irwin on 2nd March 1930, he wrote:

"It is a long letter with an intention to avoid bloodshed which may be the result of *Satyagraha*. "The British government is expending unbearable money on running the government". That the pay of Viceroy is around ₹ 21,000 per month that is ₹ 700 per day whereas the income of an average Indian is 2 *annas* (one eighth of a rupee). Thus Viceroy earns 5000 times more than an average Indian whereas in England, the Prime Minister gets only 90 times more than an average Englishman".

In this letter Gandhiji begged the Viceroy to reduce unnecessary government expenses and reduce tax which kills the poor. He requested to remove the Salt Tax. This request was rejected. As a result Gandhi took the *Dandi* March on 12 March, 1930 with 78 associates and the rest is history well-known to all.

On Education his refreshing feelings are well-known. He writes:

> "Polak and I had often very heated discussions about the desirability or otherwise of giving children an English education. It has always been my conviction that Indian parents who train their children to think and talk in English from their infancy betray their children and country. They deprive them of the spiritual and social heritage of the nation and render them unfit for the service of the country… I made a point of always talking to my children in Gujarati" (Autob. p. 287).

His views on work had a spiritual dimension. A follower of the Gita, Gandhiji always remained cheerful in difficult and stressful situations. The Gita repeats importance of cheerful and calm disposition at many places (प्रसन्न चेतसो 2-65 प्रसन्नात्मा 18-54). He dedicated all his works to God and considered work as a prayer to God. We ought to recall two verses of the Gita which give us a peep into his philosophy of work: "Man attains highest perfection by worshipping God through his work (18.46) and a *karmayogi* performs actions shaking off attachment and egoism for the sake of self-purification (5.11)."

स्वकर्मणा तमभ्यर्च्य सिद्धि विन्दति मानव (18-46)

योगिनः कर्म कुर्वन्ति संग त्यक्त्वा आत्मशुद्धये (5-11)

One *sloka* of the Gita (2.48) describes him adequately:

योगस्थ: कुररू कर्माणि संगंत्यक्त्वा धनंजय
सिद्धियसिद्धयो समो भूत्वा समत्वंयोग उच्यते।

Means and End were never two separate things, for Gandhiji. Only noble means can get the noble end. Undertaking any means to achieve an end was totally a foreign idea to Gandhiji.

Conclusion

We propose to conclude this educational effort by offering a concluding statement. Offering a concluding statement is difficult but it deserves our efforts. A teacher teaches by instruction and example. Gandhiji's instructions are contained in 100 volumes which is the world's largest collection of a man's ideas and message. Gandhiji taught us by his life. "My life is my message", was the true and brief expression of his philosophy. He developed faith in an uncertain life. He "incurred", himself to an uncertain life. खबर नहीं इस जुग में पल की, समझ मन को जाने कल की.

His concept of *Satyagraha* (सत्याग्रह) and Sarvodaya (constructive programmes), his concept of "Support the good and oppose the evil", his seven social ills must become the polar star both for teachers and students. As an individual he showed us the way that with, determination (*Samkalp*) and collaboration one can change "circumstances".

In the following four verses of Nathudanji Maheyaria, knowing my limitations, I have not provided English renderings. The couplet along with its extended explanation is given.

- देव समंदर मथिया हार गया मथ मथ्थ।
  बिन श्रम भारत के मिल्यो थू गांधी अमरथ॥

This verse (*doha*) requires knowledge of Hindu mythology. To obtain rare things like nectar and Goddess of wealth and twelve other things, Gods and devils (*asur*) churned the ocean. They obtained nectar. The poet says both *devas* and *asurs* did immense labour to churn the ocean to obtain nectar. This country, Bharat, without undertaking any labour got the nectar in the form of Gandhi.

- गांधी चादर राज री जो अरजुन लेतो ओढ़।
  बिन भारत हहथनापुरी कैरव जातो छोड़॥

The poet, Nathu Singh Mahiyaria, imagines, had Arjuna worn the *chadar* of Gandhiji the Kauravs would have left Hasthinapuri without undertaking the 18 days war known as Mahabharat.

- स्टेच्युघड़ावा की हुवे खरजो लाख करोड़।
  गांधी ने विधनाघड्यो (ने) टांकी दीधी तोड़॥

The poet reflects deeply on creation of statues of Mahatma Gandhi. The poet observes that we may spend a lakh or hundred lakh with no avail. Gandhi was created by God himself and having done the act of creation of Gandhiji, the Almighty broke off his chisel.

- कासपसुत अरू करम सुत कर परकास अपूर।
  साथे दिल्ली आंथिया नभ रा धररा सूर॥

The sun, son of Kasip, and the son of Karam Chand after giving immense light set down (in Delhi); the one the hero of the sky the other the hero of the land.

□

References

Abdul Kalam, APJ (2003) *Ignited Minds,* New Delhi, Penguin Books.

Andrews, C.F. (2006) *Mahatma Gandhi: His Life and Ideas* New Delhi Second Jaico Impression.

Bandyopadhay, P. (1994) *Sarojani Naidu*, Calcutta, Anglia Books.

Bhattacharya, S. (2001) *The Mahatma and the Poet*, New Delhi National Book Trust 2nd Reprint.

Bottery, M & Wright, N. (2000) *Teachers and the State London*, Rontledge.

Capra, F. (1996) *The Web of Life*, Flamingo.

Chattopadhyaya, D.P. (2001) *Societies, Cultures and Ideologies* Mumbai, Bhartiya Vidya Bhawan.

Collins, L. & Lapierre, D. (1993) *Freedom at Midnight* N. Delhi, Vikas Pub. House.

Coombs, P.H. (1968) *The World Education Crisis: A System Analysis* New York, Oxford University Press.

Coombs, P.H., Prosser, R.C. and Ahmed M. (1973) *New Paths to Learning*, New York International Council for Educational Development.

Fisher, Louis (2010) *The Story of Gandhi* New Delhi, Sasta Sahitya Mandal.

Freire, Paulo (1970) *Pedagogy of the Oppressed*, New York Continuum.

Galbraith, J.K. (1983) *Essays from the Poor to the Rich*, Bombay, Bhartiya Vidya Bhawan.

Gandhi, M.K. (1998) *Hind Swaraj or Indian Home Rule*, Ahmedabad Navajivan Twelfth Reprint.

Gandhi, M.K. (2004) *An Autobiography or The Story of My Experiments with Truth*, Ahmedabad, Navajivan Pub. House

Gandhi, M.K. (2010) *Gita Mata* New Delhi, Sasta Sahitya Prakashan in Hindi.

Husen Torsten (1974) *The Learning Society* London, Methuen and Co.

Hutchins, R.M. (1970) *The Learning Society* London, Penguin Books.

Illich, Irvin (1970) *Deschooling Society* New York, Harper and Row.

Iyer, Raghavan (2006) *The Essential Writings of Mahatma Gandhi* New Delhi, Oxford University Press, 15th impression.

Mujib, M. (1972) *Dr. Zakir Hussain: A Biography*, New Delhi National Book Trust.

Nanda, B.R. (1958) *Mahatma Gandhi: A Biography* Oxford University Press.

Narasimhaiah, C.D. (2003) *Western Images of India in Literature* NCERT RIE Mysore.

Narrulah, S. and Naik, J.P. (1951) *A History of Education during the British Period*, Second Edition, Bombay, Macmillan.

NCTE (1999) *Gandhi on Education* New Delhi NCTE.

Nehru, Jawaharlal (1989) *An Autobiography*, Oxford University Press, Eighth impression.

Pojman, L.P. (1998) *Environmental Ethics* Wadsworth, Pub. Co.

Reimer, E. (1971) *School is Dead* London, Doubleday and Co.

Rolland Romain (2008) *Mahatma Gandhi: Life and Philosophy* Allahabad Lok Bharati Pub. Paperback.

Salamutullah and Qudri, A.W.B. (1999) *Dr. Zakir Hussain*, New Delhi NCTE.

Sahare, M.L. (1988) *Dr. Bhimrao Ambedkar: His Life and Work* New Delhi, NCERT.

Shanker, R. (1993) *The Story of Gandhi* New Delhi, Children's Book Trust.

Steele, T & Taylor, R. (1994) "Against Modernity: Gandhi and Adult Education", *International Journal of Lifelong Education*, 13.1, pp. 33-42.

Sykes, Marjorie (2009) *The Story of Nai Taleem*, New Delhi, NCERT.

Terchek, R.J. (2000) *Gandhi Struggling for Autonomy* New Delhi Vistaar Publications.

UNESCO (1972) *Learning to Be*; Paris, Unesco (Chair Edgar Faure).

UNESCO (1996) *Learning: The Treasure Within Report to UNESCO of the International Commission on Education for the 21st Century* Paris Unesco Publishing.

UNESCO (2001) *Medium Term Plan 2002-2007* Paris, Unesco International Institute for Educational Planning.

WCEFA (1990) *World Declaration on Educational for All*, Jomtien, Thailand.

Whitehead, A.W. (1970) *The Aims of Education and other Essays* London Ernest Benn Ltd. 7th Edition.

World Education Report (1998) *Teachers and teaching in a Changed World*; Paris, Unesco.

□□□